HOT TIPS
FOR
REAL ESTATE INVESTORS

*A lady who made $1,000,000
by using leverage
shares her secrets*

by

AQLIM BARLAS

*Revised and expanded with a
40 page supplement
by*

ROBERT STUART THOMSON

GODWIN BOOKS

For information write to:
GODWIN BOOKS
P.O. Box 4781, Vancouver, B.C. V6B 4A4
Tel. (604) 988-2407 Fax (604) 984-9821
To order copies, see last page

Our tel. no. is 604 988 2407

Canadian Cataloguing in Publication Data

Barlas, Aqlim
        Hot tips for real estate investors

Includes index.
ISBN 0-9696774-4-8

        1. Real estate investment. I. Thomson,
Robert Stuart, 1940 II. Title.
HD1382.5.B37 1993 332.63'24 C93-091856-8

PREFACE TO THE 1995 EDITION

Most of last year I spent writing about real estate for British Columbia's largest daily newspaper, *The Vancouver Sun*. During that time, the book you now hold in your hand landed on my desk. Lucky me. Lucky you.

Here, artfully transcribed by co-author Dr. Robert Thomson, is the inspiring story of Aqlim Barlas, a new Canadian from Pakistan who in 1984 found herself in Surrey, British Columbia, with a broken marriage and without assets. Since then she has bought eight houses and four condos, has amassed surprisingly sizable equity, and has built herself a new life.

How she managed this you will find explained step by step, complete with pictures of her various properties. As Barlas describes her progress she drops her hot tips. Pearls of wisdom is closer to the truth, but not to quibble.

As you read this book you will learn how to find the right realtor, find property below market value, use comparables, evaluate locations, find a partner, borrow on equity, re-negotiate mortgages, buy with no money down, and much more. More to the point, you will come away with a sense that you too can enjoy similar success investing in real estate.

Although Aqlim Barlas' personal and financial growth is taking place in the Vancouver suburb of Surrey, you are about to discover practical advice which is eminently applicable right here, right now, wherever you are. Good luck!

Roderick MacDonald, *Vancouver, April 1995.*

MAIL FROM OUR READERS

"Your book is easy to read. It took me only two hours to get through it. I have applied the knowledge profitably, especially what you write about house number one. Your book is right up there with Tyler Hicks' and Robert Allan's Nothing Down for the '90s! *(Mr. J. B., San Diego)*

"I've looked at every real estate book in the Seattle Public Library. Yours is easily the best. The clearest, the most useful (. . .)." (Mr. M. M., Seattle).

"Thank you for sending HOT TIPS. I enjoyed it so much that I am sending for one more copy to give to my son who is thinking of buying his first apartment. HOT TIPS will be his guide, I'm sure." (Mrs. H. H., New Westminster, British Columbia).

"I gave your book to a friend in England and he bought low using your starting offer guidelines. I'm convinced HOT TIPS works in any country." (Mr. L. Mills, Kingston, Ontario).

"Thanks for HOT TIPS. It taught me how to evaluate my target market and with this knowledge I bought two houses below market value. I took courage from Aqlim's example. It's easy to learn when you follow in her footsteps." (Ms. M. W., Windsor, Ontario)

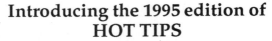

Introducing the 1995 edition of
HOT TIPS
(revised, expanded), plus a note to our American readers

HOT TIPS first appeared in 1993 and has now sold 5,000 copies. *It is officially a Canadian best seller.*

The 1995 edition which you are looking at is even better. It contains 50% new, useful material: ten pages on Aqlim's three latest deals with important lessons on incorporating, negotiating, and house inspecting. Then a whole new section: HOT TIPS FROM THOMSON'S NETWORK. "Eight smart ways to raise money" includes reverse mortgages, the 5% down program, vendor take-backs and an innovative property management scheme. Anyone can profit from this information, but *we think in particular that it will be useful to young people who, thanks to these strategies, will be able to buy property in the harsh economic climate of the '90s.* There's more. Good advice on:

- when to buy
- which areas to invest in
- how to find the right realtor
- how to find a good deal
- how to make an astute opening offer
- how to use leverage
- how to choose tenants
- how to tailor-make your rental agreement form
- what to read (only two journals!) in order to understand the market.

And welcome to our American readers! You might be interested to know that Aqlim first got bitten by the property bug while watching Scarlett rhapsodizing about her family estate in *Gone With The Wind.* Amazing how influential a good movie can be!

Will our 'tips' work for Americans? Indeed they will, because tactics is an international word and the psychology of good negotiating is the same everywhere. Besides, the differences between real estate in the U.S.A. and Canada are slight. In the U.S.A. you have "escrow" companies; in Canada there are no such institutions. The conveyancing lawyer holds the deposit in trust. Also, in most states notaries cannot do conveyancing the way notaries do in Canada. I am sure you will find HOT TIPS clear and relevant. Good hunting!!

Robert Stuart Thomson, Ph.D.
Editor/Author, Godwin Books.

4

TABLE OF CONTENTS

5

THE FOLLOWING IS NEW MATERIAL FOR THIS REVISED AND EXPANDED EDITION

MORE HOT TIPS FROM THOMSON'S NETWORK OF EXPERTS

Since 1984 Aqlim Barlas
has bought eight houses and
sold two. She has bought
four condos and sold two.
She has bought with no
money down. She has gone in
50-50 with a friend. She has
gone in 50-50 with her realtor.
She has become an expert in
property values and probably
knows the value of houses in
Newton (a suburb of Vancouver)
better than most local realtors.
How did she do this and
what other tricks did she learn?

I am eager to find out . . .

I am interviewing Aqlim in the living room of her second house. It is a bright April afternoon, and we can see the North Shore mountains, blue in the distance.

This is a most attractive house you have, Aqlim. That view of the North Shore mountains is spectacular.

Yes, I love the mountains.

You seem to have been travelling a lot in the past few years. How do you do it?

I wasn't always able to live this way, I can tell you. It's only since I've been involved in real estate that I've been able to afford things like this. Ten years ago I lost my home and my marriage and I was living in a one bedroom apartment. Using orange boxes for tables. Almost everything I had was a gift of the staff at the school (Beagle Junior Secondary) where I taught English as a second language.

That seems incredible now but before you tell us a little more about your background, can you tell your readers what you want to deal with in this book?

My main objective is to share with my readers the very valuable lessons which I've gleaned from buying and selling houses and condos. If readers follow my guidelines and adapt them to their own circumstances, they stand to make a lot of money. And these are not just theories; they are principles which have been tested in the marketplace. They really work.

8

So why don't we start with my first house (p. 12) and then look closely at all of my other transactions? We can discuss what I learnt as we go along and print in *bold script* the main things that I learnt.

That sounds good. Before we do, can you tell us how you first got the idea of buying property?

It's quite ironic how it started. It was just after my marriage broke up (1983) and real estate was the furthest thing from my mind. One evening I was chatting with a stranger at a party and he advised me to buy one house a year if I wanted to make some real money. Actually, I thought that he was a bit of a joker and at that time I was the last person in the world to believe that I would end up not only following his advice but even going a few steps further.

The irony is that he himself didn't do well at all. In fact, today he lives in a shabby basement suite which he rents from someone. Anyhow, this chance encounter planted an idea in my brain and I started to think about investing in real estate. In the fall of 1983 I started to put thoughts into action. I was renting an apartment at that time and realized all too well how much money I was throwing away every month. The more I thought about owning my own place, the better I liked the idea.

Something else happened about this time. I was watching *Gone With the Wind* for about the fourth time and there seemed to be a message for me in that scene where Scarlett O'Hara thanks heaven for her land even though her house and the surrounding area has been ravaged by the Northern troops. I find that little scene so moving and inspiring! I vowed then that one day I would have my own house and land.

How is it that you were on your own?

My marriage had reached the point where I had to move out for my own survival. However, I don't want to discuss that. It's over and the past is past.

9

Would you say that being a Pakistani woman had anything to do with your going into real estate and doing well at it?

Yes, for at least three reasons: my family upbringing, the political climate of Pakistan, and my marriage.

I grew up in an atmosphere of love and understanding. A large, close family. A lot of intelligent, refined conversation. Servants. Private school. Chaperones. University. This kind of upbringing gave me a lot of inner strength which has stood me in good stead all my life.

Growing up in Pakistan also had an impact. The political instability (military coups, political leaders jailed and executed), and the general climate of danger (illegal arrests, torture, etc.) create an atmosphere in which people are willing to take financial risks. It may seem strange, but it's true. Your attitude becomes: "Things are dangerous and unstable, so why not take a chance? Let's go for it! What have I got to lose?" When it comes to real estate speculation, a bit of the devil-may-care attitude comes in handy.

As to my marriage, I should have listened to my father's advice but I was headstrong, defied his wishes, and eloped. My marriage turned out to be a very repressive one. I was not allowed to express in public an opinion different from my husband's. Nor was I allowed to meet with women friends on my own. I was not even permitted to have my own pocket money. And this is just the tip of the iceberg. I could say lots on this topic but I would prefer not to. Let's just say that going through a marriage of this kind can make you very determined to obtain your freedom. And once you do obtain your freedom, you want to utilize it in such a way that you'll acquire lots of money and the freedom that money brings.

So, yes, my background has had a great deal to do with what I've become. It is very strange, but now I think back on it, it seems that the very forces of repression brought something very positive into my life: they impelled me to want to learn to be strong and independent.

I can tell you that I feel very strongly about equal rights

for women although I hasten to add that I like men and I am certainly not a radical feminist. Nevertheless, I dislike men who abuse their power and one day I am going to write a series of articles about my experiences and have them published in a Pakistani newspaper. I will feel very good about myself if I can contribute something along these lines. For the same reason I feel good about your publishing this book—it might help some women to free themselves, empower themselves.

> *Best amongst you (men) is he who is good to his wife."*
>
> *(The Koran, 4:19)*

I hope that it does too. But what you have said about repressive men applies to men in many cultures. There are such men in Canada too. Would you say that abusive male chauvinists are more common in Pakistan than in Canada?

I would say that there is a much higher percentage of such males in Pakistan. Just a small anecdote will give you an idea of the general level of violence and macho thinking in my native country. I remember when I was a girl we moved into a neighborhood which placed us across the street from a prison. The screams of the inmates being beaten at night was horrifying. My father, who was a kind and fair man, complained to the prison authorities about this. When he did, they told him that he was too kind and they laughed at him sarcastically. Needless to say, they changed nothing so we chose to move.

To get back to your real estate activities, what was your first house like?

I bought my first house in March 1984. It was like a first love. Nicely decorated. Four bedrooms, three bathrooms. They were asking $89,000.

I had only $5,000 but I needed $15,000 for the down payment. No commercial bank would lend me the $10,000 so I looked into alternatives. Fortunately the British Columbia Government at that time was offering first time buyers mortgage money at 10% and I was able to scrape together the down payment. Looking back, I now see that I was wise to persist in seeking a solution to the down payment problem. I was also learning to ask the right questions and to find alternative courses of action when confronted by seemingly impossible problems.

HOUSE NO. 1
66A Ave., Surrey. Note the narrow lot.

Physical details about house No. 1:

- small lot (45 ft. wide by 90 ft. deep)
- 2 storeys, 1600 square feet of living area
- 4 bedrooms and 3 bathrooms
- wood burning fireplace in living room
- washer, dryer

— family room in the basement
— carport

Financial summary of house No. 1:

Asking price:	$89,000
Aqlim paid:	$79,000
Down payment:	$15,000
Mortgage:	+ $64,000
Total:	$79,000
Rented out for:	$750
Monthly mortgage payments:	− $580
Net gain per month:	$170

Interestingly, after I bought this house the owners got very upset with their real estate agent for not advising them better. They even approached me to see if I would cancel the contract on humanitarian grounds! The lady in particular was very upset. I thought the matter over and decided that although their suffering was regrettable, they were still responsible for their own actions.

In real estate you have to assume that the other person has thought very carefully before signing anything. It's a tough business and you can't afford to be sentimental.

> *Everyone will gladly talk about the weather or real estate but no one really understands either completely."*
> *(Lord Belfast)*

My realtor told me that the bank had assessed the house at $89,000, which confirmed my impression that it was priced low. I have discovered since then that in this price range (approximately $100,000) the bank's estimates are about $5,000 lower than what the house is actually worth.

I lived in this house for five weeks before renting it out. I moved so soon because I felt insecure living there.

13

Through a newspaper ad I found some excellent tenants who painted the place and put up wallpaper. Why did they fix the place up? Well, I think they felt a bit sorry for me because I was a lady from a distant part of the world who was living alone and struggling.

Then two sisters moved in. They were good tenants too. Meticulous. They made a lot of improvements. In brief, I rented out this place for 3 1/2 years before selling it for $93,000 in 1988.

How big was the mortgage? How much of the mortgage did the rent pay off?

It was for $64,000 at 10%, which works out to about $580 a month, so the extra $170 which I received every month paid for incidentals like insurance on the house, property taxes and upkeep expenses. *(Note: in order to streamline things we have omitted in the financial summaries, property taxes and upkeep expenses—paint, faulty appliances, etc.—although of course they do exist.)*

Do you think that you were a good judge of people (as to their being suitable tenants) or were you lucky, or both?

I'm a good judge of people but I think I've been lucky too.

How did you advertise for people?

I preferred to look for people who put their own "wanted to rent" ad in the paper. I found that these people tended to be serious and reliable. Sometimes I'd get a long distance call from someone who was planning to move to Surrey and was looking for a three bedroom house or whatever. I didn't hesitate to phone such people back because the very fact that they had phoned long distance indicated that they were serious and responsible. Apart from that I would put an ad in *The Vancouver Sun* or *The Surrey Leader,* and I have had good results with both newspapers.

Were there any tip-offs in the 'wanted to rent' ads that the ad had been inserted by the type of person who would make a desirable tenant?

Yes. I'm usually impressed by someone who says that s/he is looking for a nice clean house or that s/he will look after it well. Usually people don't bother saying things like this unless they mean it. Besides, most irresponsible people wouldn't think of saying things like this anyway.

Sometimes a little detail clues you in. For instance, one pair of good tenants had advertised right up front that their child was allergic to dust and needed a very clean house. I suppose that people who really care about their kids tend to care about their houses too. In general I favor senior citizens and, of course, people with solid jobs.

Where were you living for the 3 1/2 years that the house on 66A Ave. was being rented out?

I was living in an apartment. In March, 1987 I bought the house where we're sitting having this chat right now (77A Avenue).

What?! You bought this huge house and you had hardly begun to pay off the first house (66A Avenue)! How did that come about?

Well, I was living in an apartment, which was convenient in a way because I was going through a lot of stress during my marital breakup and it was good not to have to worry about the upkeep of a house. However, about this time my mother came to visit me from Pakistan. With me, my son and my mother living together in a 2 bedroom apartment, conditions were very cramped.

Mother suggested that I buy another house. I couldn't move into the house on 66A Avenue because I had signed a one year's lease with the tenants. Mother asked me why I didn't buy another house. I told her that I didn't have the money. She said that that shouldn't be a problem and she arranged to have my brother and my sister help me out with the down-payment. They kindly came up with $10,000 but this was still not enough. I needed another $5,000, so I took out my Chargex card.

You actually used a Chargex card to take care of a big chunk of a mortgage?

Yes, it was the only thing I could do if I was going to buy this second house. All the banks I had gone to had refused to give me a loan and it was only several years later that I discovered I could have received a loan from a credit union. However, at this point I was a real novice. So I went to the bank and simply told them that I needed a cash advance. Fortunately they didn't ask any questions. I had to pay about 16% interest on this advance.

It was a very daring step I took but this second house had great possibilities. I turned the downstairs area (which is large: over 1500 square feet) into a one-bedroom suite very quickly and rented it out to cover the extra expenses (like the Chargex bill!).

People who accept conventional wisdom might think that I was foolish to take out such a large amount on my Visa, what with the high interest rates. I disagree. The thing I've learned is that *if ever you find a dynamite real estate deal, and you know that you can't help but make money on it, it is foolish not to do everything in your power to raise the cash.* You might feel uncomfortable with the debt or element of risk but you feel even worse if you don't act and you watch someone else make a nice profit on the transaction which you never made.

By the way, the asking price of the house was $110,000, which was already low, and I paid only $103,000.
There were some major problems just the same, but one learns. One day the washing machine in the basement

---

In real estate you make your money when you buy low." (a realtor's saying)

---

flooded on me and drenched the whole downstairs area. Also the exhaust on the dryer didn't work and when I turned it on every room in the house steamed up. Nothing seemed to work.

The people who sold me the house had done a real number on me. When they left they took all the keys with them, so I had to phone a locksmith to get into the house. Can you imagine! They also ran off with all the good appliances and left defective ones in their place. Not to mention the drapes and the blinds. Vanished! It was an ugly surprise.

They never would have got away with this if I had known then what I know now about the law. A person who buys property has a year during which s/he can go after the seller and legally repossess any property that has been illegally removed. This applies to things like appliances, blinds, and so on. Well, live and learn!

Anyway, enough of that! It's a beautiful house. Here's a photograph from the street.

HOUSE NO. 2

77A Ave., Surrey (Aqlim's current residence). Note the living room view windows in the top center – the ceilings are 14 ft. high. The tall tree at the back of the house shades a large sundeck (see photo, p. 19).

Living room (note the high ceilings). You can see the North Shore mountains from these windows.

Physical details about house No. 2:

- lot size: 66 ft. wide by 123 ft. deep
- 3000 square feet of living room
- 14 foot vaulted ceilings in a vast (30 ft. by 20 ft.) living room/dining room
- 14 foot fireplace made of volcanic rock
- panoramic view of the North Shore mountains from the living room
- large raised deck off the kitchen. This deck is sheltered by an 80 foot fir tree (see photo.)
- lounge with large fireplace in the basement
- also in the basement and separate from this lounge: a large (1200 sq. ft.) self-contained suite which brings in about $700 a month
- on the negative side, the house was filthy and had been neglected. It needed a lot of work and new paint

Financial summary of house No. 2:

Asking price:	$110,000
What Aqlim paid:	$103,000

Down payment:	$15,000
Mortgage:	+ $88,000
Total:	$103,000

Suite rented for: $700 per month
Monthly mort. payments:$1200
Net loss: $500 (which you could consider Aqlim's own rent)
Estimated current market value of house: $260,000

The following photo was taken from the kitchen door looking out onto the large deck. Surrey is a superb place to be
on a sunny summer afternoon.

This house was on the market a few months ago with an
asking price of $259,000. I'm pretty sure I could have made
close to that figure on it but I decided that I liked the house
too much to sell so I took it off the market.

**I sure like this house. What words would describe
it? Certainly elegant. Stately. What are the features
of it that attracted you?**

The 14 foot vaulted ceiling. The panorama of the North Shore mountains which you see right out those windows. That huge fireplace which is made of volcanic rock. And this enormous dining-room/living room.

Let's go back to 1988. You have bought this house (77A Avenue) with a down payment of $15,000 and you have another house (66A Avenue) which you rent out on a yearly lease. What happened next?

In 1988 I sold house No. 1. I had paid $79,000 for it. I sold it for $93,000 and made $13,000. The realtor was a close friend and I negotiated a special commission. Property was going up swiftly at that time (see graph, p. 42) and afterwards I realized that I could have made quite a bit more on it if I'd waited. I was a bit annoyed with myself but I soon realized that it is useless to dwell on such things. I took the money I made and paid off my debts. I also bought two more houses.

Sale of house No. 1:

Selling price:	$93,000
Aqlim paid:	– $79,000
Profit:	$14,000
Equity:	+ $8,000
Total profit:	= $22,000
(Less commission of $2,000)	

By "equity" here we mean the amount of Aqlim's mortgage which the renters paid off during their tenancy. When the house is sold, the bank is paid off the amount still owing on the mortgage (in this case, $56,000). When a mortgage is paid off this way, you have to pay a penalty to the bank. One way to avoid this penalty is to transfer the mortgage to another property, which is what Aqlim did.

So you bought two more houses. A bold move.

**Sounds like you turned your annoyance with your-
self into something positive by becoming aggressive
in real estate. What were these houses like?**

Before I tell you about the two houses, I want to tell you
something about realtors and my realtor in particular. I met
mine, Dick Balchen, through the newspaper. He looked
reliable and honest from his photograph and his ad con-
tained several listings and "solds," which indicated that he
was a real go-getter. I arranged to interview him. And, you
know, right away I felt comfortable with him. He listened
well and seemed to reflect thoughtfully before he spoke.
This inspired confidence. Most important, he was very
good with a computer.

It is important to find a really competent realtor who will
work with you. Dick is just that. We trust each other and
have operated very much as a team. He knows that he can
count on me for a lot of business so he is flexible about
commissions (which I think is reasonable). I in turn can
count on him to tip me off whenever he hears of a really
good deal.

Dick also gives me access to a truly wonderful source of
information: The Multiple Listing Service Sales Book (this
is different from the MLS Listings Book). The "Sales" book
tells you how much houses have actually sold for. It lists in
ascending order of price all of the houses that sold last
month in whatever district you're interested in. A great
way to check out comparable prices! Now when I see a
house that I want to make an offer on, I get a good idea of
where to pitch my offer by (1) looking up recent comparable sales in the MLS Sales Book and (2) asking Dick to run
a check for comparables on his computer.

For instance, when I went to sell house #1, I used the
computer to find out the selling price of comparable houses in the area. This gave me confidence that my price was
right. Any computer-literate realtor can get these stats for
you, by the way. S/he can also spot excellent deals on the
computer even before they are posted at the real estate
office. This is worth keeping in mind . . . Which comparables? Ask your realtor for help. I usually have mine punch

21

in location, time frame, price range (you have to use trial and error to get this right, otherwise you get too many or too few comparables), and number of bedrooms. Comparables like these will give you a good idea of the market, whether you are buying or selling. Be sure to drive out and actually look at the comparables. This really helps.

If I'm interested in buying a place, I always ask Dick to check out its price history. How many times has it sold and for how much? More important: When did the present owner buy it, and for how much? What kind of mortgages are owing on it? I'll weigh all of this before I make an offer.

Anyhow, to get back to house #1, I checked the comparables and was confident that my asking price was about right. House #1 took only two weeks to sell.

How much did you say you cleared on house No. 1?

I cleared about $22,000 if you include the equity which I built up by decreasing the mortgage. However, as you

---

"There are three kinds of people: those who make things happen, those who watch things happen, and those who wonder what happened."

(Source unknown)

---

suggested, I was a bit annoyed with myself for not making more on this sale and I was in the kind of mood which caused me to pounce on the next two houses.

That's pretty spectacular. How did that come about?

Let me tell you about the two houses. One house was on 80th Ave. and 144th St. (let's call it house No. 3).

HOUSE NO. 3

80th Ave. It's hard to see, but the living room window is broken. The tenants must have been partying. Anyhow, they don't seem to mind the added ventilation.

Physical details about house No. 3:

- large lot (66 ft. by 126 ft.) with a fenced backyard
- 1100 square feet of floor space
- 3 bedroom rancher
- remodeled kitchen
- 2 skylights in bathroom
- laundry room off the kitchen

Financial summary of house No. 3:

Asking price:	$79,000
What Aqlim paid:	$75,000
Down payment:	$7,000
Mortgage:	+ $68,000 (11%)
Total:	$75,000
Rented out for:	$700
Monthly mort. payments:	$750
Net loss:	$50 a month

This house was owned by a real estate agent who was moving to Penticton. He was asking $79,000. I paid $75,000 for it, which I think was not a bad deal. I decided what to offer by first checking out the comparable sales for that area of Surrey in the two previous months. Doing this bolsters your confidence although of course you have to use your common sense, intuition, etc. as well.

Another important thing which I learned to consider is the motivation of the seller. In the above case, I was pretty sure that they'd seriously consider my offer because the realtor's wife had already moved to Penticton and he was anxious to join her. He was in a hurry to sell. Their one year mortgage had also expired and they didn't want to have to renew it or take out another. By the way, this issue of how to recognize a vendor who is in a big hurry (and is therefore likely to accept a lower offer on his/her place) is too interesting not to touch on here. From my experience and that of my friends, I would say that there are seven main scenarios:

(1) the sellers are divorcing or have had a falling out.

(2) there has been a death (or notification of a terminal illness) and someone is eager to sell for this reason.

(3) the seller is out of the country and is not well informed as to what the property is really worth.

(4) the seller has begun to feel very negative about his/her home and can't wait to move out. This kind of person will often drop the asking price for no apparent good reason.

(5) the seller has fallen in love with another place, and has put an offer on it. This offer will be accepted only if the first unit sells. If the first unit doesn't sell, the seller won't get the house s/he wants. S/he might even lose the deposit on the house if it's a non-refundable one.

(6) the seller has lost a job or for some other reason can no longer pay the mortgage every month.

(7) the listing is stale (the house has been on the market too long).

There are other scenarios, as well, of course. I have a friend who was shown a lovely apartment (with 9 foot ceilings) in the West End of Vancouver. This apartment was listed in Multiple Listing Service (realtor's book of listings) at $140,000. It was described as being 625 sq. ft. In fact the correct square footage was **740** square feet so a fair price would have been $175,000. The listing realtor (who was usually to be found in Hong Kong) had actually measured the apartment incorrectly!

The realtor who showed my friend the apartment knew this (and he apparently was the *only* realtor who knew it). He informed my friend, but unfortunately my friend didn't pounce on the deal. It was a *sure thing*. A sure way to make $20,000 very quickly because the apartment was considerably underpriced. It was a steal. *I mention this to show you that the real estate market is complex and not always logical. A lot of deals exist because of errors like this and if you keep informed you are bound to run into one.* It takes a long time in most jobs to save $20,000.

To get back to house No. 3, the mortgage I took out on it was for $68,000. This meant monthly payments of $750. I rented it out for $700 a month.

Okay, now what about the other (4th) house which you say you bought at this time (1989)?

This house is on 66A and 134th St. Here's a photo of it.

Can I interrupt you for a moment? Was this the house that you rented out to the Hell's Angels?

No, it isn't. You're thinking of house No. 3 (80th Ave.). I had some scary renters there. In the living room window they'd put up a warning sign which said, "Is there life after death? Trespass here and find out!"

(By the way, if any readers get confused about which properties we are referring to in this book, they should see page 74 for a complete summary of all the properties I've bought and sold.)

HOUSE NO. 4
The houses in this neighborhood are newer and better than those in the neighborhood of house No. 3 (see map, p. 30).

Physical details about house No. 4:

- 45 by 95 feet lot
- 1300 square feet of living space
- 3 bedroom, 2 storey with the bedrooms all upstairs
- bright living room with a fireplace
- hardwood floors in the living room/dining room
- remodeled kitchen
- family room downstairs
- covered garage

Financial summary of house No. 4:

Asking price:	$79,000
Aqlim paid:	$78,000
Down payment:	$19,500
Mortgage:	+ $58,500
Total:	$78,000
Rented out for:	$775
Mort. payment:	− $770
Net gain:	$5

I discovered this house when I was out driving around one day. (You never know when or how you're going to come across a good deal.) It was located across the street from the first house which I bought.

The owners had just lost their job. They had bought this house in the late 1970's (when prices were rising rapidly) for $109,000. They were locked into one of the outrageous mortgages that were common at that time. 18%, maybe 19%. I bought it for $78,000, which I knew was an excellent price.

Actually, to be more precise, I went in halfers with a friend from the Interior of British Columbia. I'm not sure that I would have bought this one if I had not had a partner and *I don't believe in the 'conventional wisdom' which advises you not to invest in real estate with anyone,* that you'll lose your shirt, that you'll lose your friend, that you'll end up in court, etc. To me, that's just baloney. Cynical baloney. Going in with a partner can create all kinds of opportunities.

> *"It is better to be deceived by your friends than to mistrust them."*
>
> *(Maxims of the Duke of La Rochefoucauld, a courtier at the court of Louis XIV of France.)*

There was another reason why I needed a partner to buy this house: I couldn't raise the $19,500 down payment on my own and the bank required this $19,500 down payment before they would give me a mortgage. (It is standard policy of banks to demand 35% down payment on investment property. By pooling our money my friend and I were able to buy this house.) My half of the down payment came to $9,750, which is a lot easier to raise than the full $19,500.

By the way, it is a big advantage to keep the down payment as small as possible if you are going to rent out the property because *the interest which you pay on the mortgage of rental property is tax deductible. Also, the less you put down on one property, the more you have available to invest in other property.*

This house also appealed to me because I could drive there in five minutes from my residence. This is a good thing to keep in mind, I think, if you're planning to buy a bunch of houses. *It is very convenient to live close to the properties which you buy.*

The mortgage was $58,000 and the interest was 11.5%. We rented it out for $775 a month so the rent offset the mortgage with about $5 to spare.

This fourth house was also good in that it came with some good renters. That's always something to consider. The renters who were already there stayed on for a year. They were very dependable, as were the couple who replaced them and who also stayed for a year.

Okay, Aqlim, let's pause a moment and tell your readers something about the area where you did your wheeling and dealing. Then let's summarize exactly what you did. First, where exactly is Surrey?

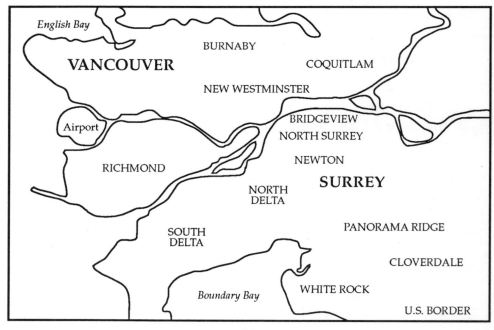

Surrey's location is best understood if you look at the above map of Greater Vancouver. One of several suburbs of Vancouver, Surrey lies southeast of it and is located just south of the Fraser River. Surrey is a rather large area (132 square miles) and has been growing at breakneck speed for the past ten years or so. It is probably the fastest growing suburb in Canada.

It is a complex area socio-economically in spite of the fact that it is the butt of a lot of British Columbian jokes which makes it sound like something out of the Ozarks and in spite of the very poor (and unfair) press which it received in a *Maclean's Magazine* article written by Jill Timson in the late 1970's. *(Editor's note, 1995: the recent episode of a vendetta murder — someone was served up in a pizza — didn't help.)*

Are all the areas of Surrey the same or does it vary?

Surrey itself is loosely divided into various areas: Whalley and Guildford in the north, Newton and Cloverdale in the centre and White Rock in the south. Each area tends to

Below: Aqlim's third house, a rancher.

Above: Newton mansion

have distinctive housing styles. At the top end of the scale are the mansions of Panorama Ridge, White Rock, and even Newton (see photo, page 29, top left). Towards the other end of the market you'll find the modest rancher like Aqlim's third house (see page 29, lower right). Most of Aqlim's property is located in the Newton area of Surrey, an area which is characterized for the most part by modest, middle of the road dwellings (see the area map on page 28). In the course of time Aqlim ventured out of this area, buying first a house in North Surrey (see page 50), then a condo in Vancouver's West End (see page 55).

To summarize, the following map traces Aqlim's steps so far.

120 ST. (SCOTT RD.)	128 ST.	136 ST. (KING GEORGE HIGHWAY)	
		C1, 2	100 AVE.
H6		**C4**	96 AVE.
			88 AVE.
	H3		80 AVE.
			72 AVE.
		H5	
	H4		
	H1		64 AVE.

Looking at the same steps with miniature photos, the pattern is as follows:

STEP 1
bought house No. 1
(66A) 1984 (May)

STEP 2
bought house No. 2
(77A) 1987 (March)

STEP 3
sold house No. 1
1988 (May)

STEP 4
bought house No. 3
(80th Ave.) 1989

STEP 5
bought house No. 4
(66th A Ave.) 1989

THE BOTTOM LINE (as of 1989):

Aqlim has bought 4 units. She has sold 1 and now owns 3. She lives in 1 of these, rents out the basement suite, and rents out the other 2. She will be making good money for two reasons: (1) in the long run prices will rise; (2) her renters are paying off her mortgages and increasing her equity. By 1989 Aqlim had already made about $40,000. because all of her mortgages had been partly paid off by her renters. The amounts which she had paid in down payments added to her equity.

To summarize the 1989 scenario in more detail:

- **House No. 1: 66A Ave. and 134A Ave.**
  Bought in June, 1984. Sold in 1988.
  Paid $79,000 (sold for $93,000)
  Brought in rent of: $750 which more than paid for monthly mortgage payments of $580.
  Net revenue generated per month was: $170.

- **House No. 2: 77A Ave. (Aqlim's current residence)**
  Bought in February 1987.
  Paid $103,000.
  Brings in rent of $700 which helps to pay for monthly mortgage payments of $1,200.
  Net revenue generated per month: –$500.
  Estimated equity (down payment plus part of mortgage paid) in this house: $20,000.

- **House No. 3: 80th Ave.**
  Bought in March 1989.
  Paid $75,000.
  Brings in rent of $700 which almost pays for monthly mortgage payment of: $750.
  Net revenue generated per month: – $50.
  Estimated equity (1989) in this house: $15,000.

- **House No. 4: 66A Ave. and 134th St.**
  Bought in March 1989 (sold for $135,000 in March, 1991).
  Paid $78,000.
  Brought in rent of: $775 which more than paid for monthly mortgage payment of $770.
  Net revenue generated per month: $5.
  Estimated equity in this house: $17,000.

Total estimated equity (amount Aqlim's share of the properties is actually worth) as of 1989: $52,000.

The following figures show clearly how the rents which Aqlim receives more or less pay off her mortgages.

	Rent Received	Mortgage Payment
HOUSE NO. 1	$750	$580
HOUSE NO. 2	$700	$1200
HOUSE NO. 3	$700	$750
HOUSE NO. 4	$775	$770
TOTAL	$2925	$3300

THE KEY TO IT ALL:
Aqlim's mortgage payments amount to $375 per month more than the various rents which she receives. However, her regular salary from teaching provides a protective cushion. Also, she lives in house No. 2 herself so she has no rent to pay. Everything is building equity.

> *"To do well in business by far the most important quality required of a person is persistence."*
>
> *(Joseph P. Cossman)*

Before we look at your next moves, can you share some of your ideas on mortgages? Also, how did you establish how much rent to charge for the houses which you were renting out?

I pretended to be a prospective tenant and checked out some prices in person. I then used this information to establish my prices. By doing this I am pretty confident about pricing my unit.

I see. That's very clever. Reminds me of Homer's Ulysses. You obviously do your homework. So you tended to charge somewhat less if the prospective tenants were reliable. Did you find by this time that your dealings with the bank had changed at all? Did you sense that you had more credibility in their eyes as you were acquiring property?

I'm not sure about that, but I did make a very valuable contact at the Scotiabank: Eileen Knight. I have taken out at least 12 mortgages, and Eileen makes every effort to get me the best rate. If she can get me prime variable, she does. I feel that I have an excellent realtor and an excellent mortgage broker. This is so important.

Did I hear correctly? Did you say that you've been through 12 mortgages? I only see 4 houses here. How is that?

Well, let's see. I bought 3 condos last year, and a house.

The pace seems to be quickening. How about if we leave mortgages for now and explore the next properties you bought? Let's go back and summarize. It's 1989 and you own three properties. You have sold one. You live in another and you rent out the other two.

Okay. The next property I bought was with the realtor himself.

How did that come about?

The house (which is near 70th Ave. and 137th St.) cost us $118,000. The down payment was $30,000 or $15,000 each. I didn't have this kind of money so I had to come up with something quickly. By asking around I discovered that I could borrow for one house by using the equity on another house as a guarantee or collateral. From the bank's point of view, if I didn't pay off the loan, they could take possession of the other house. This was the first time that I had heard about this but when I looked into it, it made sense. It certainly pays to ask questions.

How exactly do you borrow on your equity?

I went to the Scotiabank. I owed them the mortgage on house No. 3. I filled out the application and after a few formalities they gave me the money.

First, I had to pay to have house No. 3 appraised (this cost $120). Second, I had to pay a lawyer for conveyancing (this cost $600). As a result of these "formalities" the bank decided that:

(1) House No. 3, which I had bought for $75,000, was now worth $116,000.

(2) Since I owed $68,000 on the house, I had an equity of $48,000 in it. In other words, the bank reasoned that since I owned 48/116 of the house, they were quite safe in lending me $25,000 (at 8.25% rate of interest) because the house was there to back up the loan.

The bottom line is that by borrowing $25,000 on house No. 3, I got the down payment for house No. 5. *This transaction cost me money ($720) but it empowered me to take advantage of an opportunity which otherwise would have been lost forever.* There is a good lesson in this kind of thing.

Buying the house on 70th Ave. was definitely an opportunity which was not to be missed and, although I don't regret borrowing on another property to do it, I have since discovered that it is possible to buy property with nothing at all down. But more on this later! (see page 59).

House No. 5 was sold to Dick Balchen (my realtor) and me by an elderly couple who were getting tired of taking care of the large lot and looked forward to down-scaling to a condo. Dick was spending quite a bit of time trying to persuade me how good a deal the house was, so I finally said to him, "If it's such a good deal why don't you come in on it with me?" He agreed and proposed a 30% (him)/70% (me) split.

Then later on I thought, "30% is not enough. Why shouldn't he pay 50-50 so that if I sink, he will sink too?"He agreed to pay 50%.

"There is a tide in the affairs of men which,
Taken at the flood, leads on to fortune.
Omitted, all is lost in shallows and in miseries."

(Shakespeare, Julius Caesar)

Actually, it now seems like an even better investment than I thought at the time because the property which it's on has been rezoned since as "commercial" and I have heard rumors that Safeway might be interested in it. When we bought it we had no idea that this would happen but it has happened and I guess you can chalk it up to good luck. Although, come to think of it, by buying lots of property I maximized the chances that something like this would happen.

It's modest of you to call it "luck," but maybe this is a case where the old saying, "Fortune favours the brave" applies. You sound pretty brave to me.

Dealing in real estate and making fairly big decisions have developed my courage. Let me tell you an amusing story. Just after I bought my first house I went to a financial advisor who strongly advised me not to buy any more property. Several friends and acquaintances advised me in the same way. It's a good thing that I followed my instincts! But I suppose you'd like to know something about the house. Here's a photo of it:

HOUSE NO. 5

The good news is that this property has been rezoned to commercial since Aqlim bought it.

Physical details about house No. 5:

- large lot (70 ft. wide by 130 ft. deep)
- 900 square feet of floor area
- 2 bedrooms
- clean and in good condition
- appliances in excellent condition
- detached garage

Financial summary of house No. 5:

Asking price:	$128,000
What Aqlim paid:	$118,000
Down payment:	$30,000
Mortgage: + $88,000 (6.6% for 2 years)	
Total:	$118,000
House rents for:	$850
Monthly mort payment:	– $650
Net gain:	$200

(Estimated market value as of July, 1993: $175,000.)

The tenants who were already in the house stayed. They kept the place in good repair and looked after the garden. They were very reliable and gave us 12 post-dated cheques at the beginning of the year.

Do you maintain contact with your tenants? How often do you see them?

In this case I haven't had anything to do with them. In fact, I've never even met them. Dick has dropped in on them a couple of times and has told me that they are looking after things well. In general, the two most common problems are cheques bouncing and gardens not being looked after but we haven't had problems with either of these things.

I've heard that realtors have to inform the seller if they (the realtors) are the ones buying the property. Is this what you had to do in this case?

Yes, the real estate agent did tell them that he was one of the buyers and we had to sign a separate paper.

How much did you pay for the house? How much was the mortgage? etc.

We paid $118,000 and the mortgage payment came to $650 a month. We got a "prime variable" (which means that the actual interest that we pay on the mortgage varies with the fluctuations in the Bank of Canada prime rate). This is also known as a variable interest rate mortgage.

The rent brings in $850 a month so between the two of us we make $100 a month on this house. After expenses. Actually, after four months we locked in the mortgage for a two year term (I find two years is usually the ideal length for a mortgage) at 6.6%.

How does this "prime variable" interest rate work? What are the advantages to it?

This kind of interest rate fluctuates so you have to watch what the prime rate is doing. If it looks like it's going to go up, and stay up for a while, you might want to lock the mortgage in at the current rate. This kind of mortgage allows you to pay off the principal sooner than would otherwise be possible. You are allowed to pay a lump sum on it at any time and you can pay off the balance of the mortgage any time without penalty.

Although this kind of mortgage costs a little more (1/2% usually), by using it a greater percentage of your mortgage payment goes to paying off the principal.

Let's get back to your wheelings and dealings. Let's go back to 1991. In that year you sold one property and bought two more. Can you give us the details?

Yes, the property (house No. 4) which I'd bought with a friend for $79,000 we sold for $135,000.

How much profit did you actually make then?

It breaks down as follows:

Sold for:	$135,000
Aqlim and partner had bought it for:	− $79,000
Gross profit:	$56,000
Minus realtor's fee and conveyancing:	− $7,000
Net profit:	$49,000
Aqlim's share is one half:	$24,500
She also has equity from mortgage:	$3,000
Total profit:	$27,500

After paying the various expenses (notary's fee for conveyancing, real estate commission of $6,000), we shared the profits. These came to about $27,500 each. A nice reward for having trusted a friend, if you want to look at it that way. The profit money came in very handy. With it I paid off some bills, took a trip to England and to Pakistan and bought two condos.

Was this the trip from which you came back dazzling your school colleagues with emeralds?

Yes, it was. Emeralds and rubies and sapphires.

They *are* impressive. Did you have any difficulty selling the house? Did you have any difficulty getting your asking price?

No, we sold it easily enough but we got less than our asking price. We had put it on the market at $156,000 but settled for $135,000. The realtor with whom I had bought house No. 5 agreed to a $6,000 commission, which helped matters. One of the reasons why we settled for $135,000 is that there were several things that needed to be fixed in the house and instead of fixing them we agreed to a reduced price.

What happens to the mortgage when you sell a place like this? Do you ever transfer it to the buyer?

In this case we transferred the mortgage to the buyer

40

because this helped close the deal. Usually I prefer to avoid doing this and I have done it only twice (with houses 1 and 4). My reason is that as the vendor of a rental property I am held legally responsible for seeing that the mortgage payments are met by the buyer until the term of the existing mortgage expires (a good example of Canadian red tape). I prefer to avoid unnecessary risks.

So I usually bite the bullet and pay the penalty to the mortgage company upon completion of the sale. Of course there is another alternative and that is to apply the mortgage on the property which you've just sold to another property. However, the timing is very critical here and it's not likely that you are going to be able to find that good a deal in another property at such a convenient time. If you could, it would be very convenient because you could save a bundle in mortgage pay-out fees and conveyancing fees. Banks vary, by the way, as to how long they'll give you to make transfers like these. From what I've seen, Scotiabank is the most generous and allows you 90 days to transfer your mortgage.

I also notice you said that you hired a notary public rather than a lawyer.

Yes, notaries are often less expensive and they can do just as good a job as a lawyer. Provided that you shop around and find a good one.

What was your next move in real estate?

I bought a couple of condos.

That's interesting. A new kind of housing for you to get into. Can we put that on hold for a minute and explore something else? I believe that you did a B.A. (and M.A.) at the University of Lahore and that one of your majors was economics. Have you been able to apply any of the things, statistics, for instance, that you learned at university?

41

I have a master's in sociology. For my B.A. I studied English literature and Persian literature, economics, sociology and political science. But my main education comes from the street. What do you call it? – "street wise"?

What I mean is, did you ever make a detailed study of the selling price of Surrey houses?

I don't think that you can generalize about Surrey. Whalley is very different from White Rock. Even in Newton (where I have done most of my buying and selling) prices vary a great deal. I am not convinced that the graphs can show you a great deal except the overall ups and downs of the housing market. *They show you the past, but not the future.*

This graph is especially interesting to look back on because it shows you in what years the prices rose suddenly, and in what years they declined. (The jargon for this sudden dip is the so-called "market correction.") Surrey had a big "market correction" in 1990. By the way it's been rising for the past three years I'd say that a "market correction" is due. *(Editor's note, 1995: there have been several "corrections" in the past two years. Aqlim was right.)*

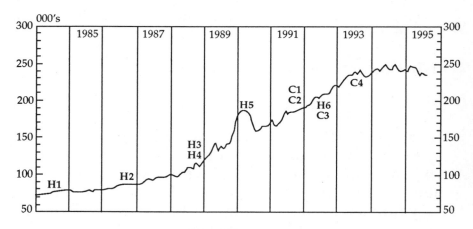

Average selling prices in Surrey.
Aqlim's purchases: H = houses; C = condos)

The overall prices dropped considerably in 1990. It is interesting to me that there was next to nothing in the newspapers about this. Anyway, it's useful to keep the idea of a possible "market correction" impacting suddenly because the thought of this possibility helps to keep you from gambling too recklessly.

Nevertheless, these ups and down's in the local real estate market didn't affect me because I had my units rented out and I was not forced to sell anything during that slump in the market. I could afford to wait and that is what I did. They say that timing is important. That is true. And part of good timing is knowing when to wait and do nothing.

I've seen a lot of people lose a lot of money by being too impatient to wait for the market to turn upwards. They panic and sell and lose heavily. There are many others who miss out on great opportunities because they are afraid to invest in real estate when the prices seem high.

Some people might study the graph above and conclude that I was just lucky to have bought most of my property when it was relatively cheap. I disagree, because when I bought my properties prices seemed to be high then too. Prices usually seem to be too high when you look at them in the present. *However, there are always bargains to be found or created by making a low bid. I think that you can make money at almost any time of the market cycle. Again, the key is to know your market. Know what the price should be.*

Anyway, for me Dick was the best advisor. For instance, at one point I was interested in buying property in the Bridgeview area. (The area just east of the King George Highway and just south of the Pattullo Bridge – see the map on p. 28.) Dick advised against it because he said that it was a bad area. Hookers. Bikers. And so on. I took his advice and avoided this area.

"60% of single Canadian women invested in some kind of real estate last year."

Dick was right. A bad area attracted a bad type of tenant. A good area tended to have a better quality of tenant. Just common sense. In a good area you can also ask for a larger rent. As a single woman I am definitely not prepared to meet and deal with tough-looking men, as I did with house No. 3. Any time I went to collect the rent there, I made sure that I had a male escort with me. I usually went with my realtor, and once you came with me yourself.

Yes, you're referring to those "Far Side" types who posted in the living room window that strange invitation to sample the after-life. Can we take an overview for a minute, Aqlim, and summarize? It seems to me that you are in this 'business' for the long haul and that you are stable. You've got a steady job with good pay.

Yes, I have a steady job teaching English as a second language at a senior high school. I also teach night school twice a week. All of this work gives me a certain amount of investment income every month. I am in real estate for the "long haul," as you say, and if there were a "market correction" I would be able to sit it out and not sell out in panic.

The real estate market is like a series of waves. You are constantly riding up on a crest but inevitably you go down into a trough. As I said, I think that Surrey is going to go down into a bit of a trough soon (as we are discussing this it is late April, 1993). Prices in Surrey have, I think, hit a peak and they can't go up forever. They are going to slide down. The alarming sign is that people can't afford the prices that are being asked right now. If the interest rate goes up, (which I think it will) property values will fall.

It will be much like what happened in Toronto last year. A lot of people there got their foot caught in the door. They thought that the prices would just keep on going, up and up and up. But that's not the way it works.

There is another influence at work, and that's people. Once a sizeable number of people decide that they are going to buy, market pressure is created and the prices go up. There is a kind of herd mentality. The same kind of thing made so many people suddenly decide to buy Japanese vehicles at high prices and avoid American vehicles even though American vehicles are often very good and are much more reasonably priced. In the same way, once a great number of people decide not to buy property, then the prices fall. It's all quite strange and unpredictable.

> **"You make money by anticipating trends, not by following them."**
> *(A truism in finance)*

Let's go back to 1991. You own the following houses: No. 2 (77A Ave.), No. 3 (80th Ave.) and No. 5 (70th Ave.). You've sold two houses and you're about to buy two others. How did you hear about them and what did you buy?

I bought two apartments. There was a "blow-out" (This is when the owner of a condo complex sells off all the units in one intensive campaign) at a complex called Carriage Lane (on 100th Ave. and approximately 137th St. in Surrey).
 My real estate agent told me about this. He said that it was going to come on the market in about a month's time and he showed me the building before the units were offered to the public. It does help to have a realtor who spots good opportunities before most other people. I bought one unit right away then another about a week later.

What were these units like?

It's an attractive complex. Three large blocks of apartments, three stories high. Wooden buildings – typically West Coast. Here's a photo of the entrance to give you an overview:

CONDO NO. 1
Entrance to Carriage Lane.

There is also an indoor recreation facility with pool tables and sauna. The grounds are attractive, with lots of lawn and flowers, and a paved access road. The complex is built on the sideslope of a bit of a ridge so the units facing west have a choice view. Especially if you're on at least the 2nd floor. I bought one of these choice units.

You can see the new "Skytrain" (Greater Vancouver "metro") station from the complex and it will be only a 5 minute walk from Carriage Lane to the Skytrain station once the station is completed. Following is a map to show you where the Skytrain will run.

At the present time (July, 1993), the Skytrain goes only as far as that part of Surrey which is closest to Vancouver (Scott Road Station). Within 10 months there will be two new Skytrain stations, one at 100th Ave. This is very close to Aqlim's condo.

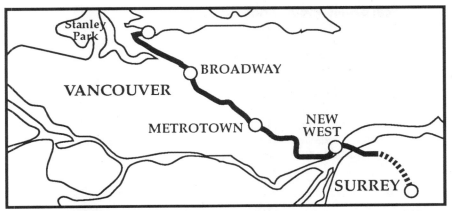

Map of Skytrain route from Vancouver to Surrey. Two new stations will be completed in early 1994. (Editor's note, 1995: they were completed but condo prices were not affected. A glut of condos on the market didn't help any.)

I was convinced that this development was going to make Carriage Lane look pretty good in the near future. By Skytrain, downtown Vancouver will be only 20 minutes away. In fact, eventually it will be faster to travel to downtown Vancouver than it would be to travel to nearby Cloverdale (an area of Surrey located to the east, only five miles away) by bus!

With a one-bedroom priced in the $70,000 range (I paid $72,900) it had to be a good deal.

100th Ave. Skytrain station under construction. Carriage Lane condos are in the background, but not really visible.

Physical details about condo No. 1:

- an attractive, spacious unit (approx. 700 sq. ft.)
- situated on the 2nd floor
- an excellent view to the west (standing on the balcony you have a great feeling of open space)
- large balcony suitable for barbecuing
- a sunken living room with wood-burning fireplace and vaulted ceiling
- appliances include a dishwasher and microwave
- secured underground parking

Financial summary of condo No. 1:

Price:	$72,900 (non-negotiable)
Down payment:	$7290
Mortgage:	+ $65,610
Total:	$72,900
Rents out for:	$600
Monthly mort. payment:	− $520
Net gain:	$80

The second unit which I bought at Carriage Lane was similar to the first except that it was on the third (top) floor, and so had an even better view. It cost $76,000.

Financial summary of condo No. 2:

Price:	$76,000
Down payment:	$7600
Mortgage:	+ $68,400
Total:	$76,000
Rents out for:	$605
Monthly mort. payment:	− $460
Net gain:	$145

After paying maintenance fees, I break even.

Both units were already tenanted – with excellent tenants – so there was nothing to do except collect the rent cheques. The second floor unit brings in $600 a month and requires monthly mortgage payments of $520. The third floor unit rents out for $605 a month and requires mortgage payments of $460 a month. As a result, both units operate in the black and they bring in a total of $225 each month.

When I first bought these units I tried to get $650 a month in rent but neither tenant could afford it and since both were good tenants with a proven track record I decided not to raise the rent. One tenant is a tutor; the other one works in the Department of Revenue. Anyway, it's better to settle for a little less money if you've already got a good tenant who can't or won't pay any more.

There was no choice on the mortgage and this is often the case with a blow-out. Everyone had to deal with the Royal Bank. However, last year (1992) when the mortgages came up for renewal I transferred both of them to the Scotiabank for two reasons.

First, the Royal Bank was charging a renewal fee of $85, which I considered an unnecessary rip-off. (They already make too much money on your mortgages.) I asked them to drop this fee, but they refused so I told them, "I'll take my business elsewhere." This was a pleasure.

Second, the Scotiabank was giving me a better rate (7.7% locked in for two years whereas the Royal Bank's rate was 8.5%). It's always wise to find out if any other financial institution is offering a better deal. I never hesitate to make switches like this because it's my money!

I know it takes time to do this kind of thing, but if you are interested in making money in real estate you have to be ready to spend time at it. When you read about the places I've bought, it might not sound like too much work, but you must remember that for every place I bought there were probably a hundred others that I read about, fifty that I heard about and twenty others that I actually looked at. This all takes a great deal of time, energy, determination and positive thinking.

How did you get such a good deal from the Scotiabank?

Well, I told the loans officer that she should get me a good deal because I was taking out two mortgages. She phoned Toronto and explained the situation. It didn't take Toronto long to come up with the 7.7% figure.

7.7% is an excellent rate. It seems to me that you are persistent and very good at playing one mortgage institution against the other. This is something that I haven't heard of many people doing but clearly you do your homework and you shop for mortgages. How do you do this?

First I look in the financial section of the newspaper, then I go from bank to bank and find out what their rates are. I mean I find out what the rates *really* are when the bank takes into account that I might be buying a couple of mortgages for two different dwellings. I make a deal with one of the banks when I find what I think is a desirable interest rate. I have found that some of the banks (Canadian Imperial Bank of Commerce, the Royal Bank) are not interested in even *listening* to what their competitors are offering so I don't waste much time with this kind of attitude.

Okay, we're up to January of 1992. What was your next deal?

I bought a house for $145,000 (it was listed for $155,000). It is in North Surrey, which is a few miles out of my normal territory (photos opposite).

Physical details of house No. 6:

- located in North Surrey on north-facing slope so it has an excellent view of the Fraser River and New Westminster beyond it (see map on page 28, top left)
- large lot (65 ft. by 130 ft.) with huge trees, very private, fenced
- 1150 square feet of floor area
- 3 bedrooms, family room
- separate garage with a family room in its loft
- large patio looking out onto a shady back yard

House No. 6 (North Surrey). Nicely treed with a panoramic view of the Fraser River to the north.

The back yard of house No. 6. Shaded and secluded.

Financial summary of house No. 6:

— Asking price:		$155,000
— Aqlim paid:		$145,000
— Down payment:		$25,000
— Mortgage:	+	$120,000
— Total:		$145,000
— House rents for:		$925
— Monthly mort. payment:		$950
— Net loss:		$25

I paid $25,000 down, which left a mortgage of $120,000. This works out to $950 a month. At the moment this house is bringing in $925 a month in rent. I had to get rid of the tenants who were there because they couldn't afford the rent. The woman who is there now can afford it and is reliable.

This house was found for me by my realtor, Dick, who had noticed it and thought it was a good deal. (Just for the record, it was not his listing.)

It seems to me that a good realtor is worth a lot of money.

Yes, Dick is an excellent realtor. He knows the area (Surrey-Delta) very well and he has a sharp eye for a good deal. He never tries to use pressure tactics with me and we have a lot of trust for each other.

He knows that I rely on him but I don't put all of my eggs into one basket. I make it clear that I too am keeping my eyes open and that I am always looking around for a good deal. So my energies are not wasted. I don't want my realtor to think that I am solely dependent on him. If I did this he would probably get too relaxed, which would not be good.

How much time do you think you spend in the average week on real estate speculation and property management?

Every day I read the want ad section, "Homes for sale by owners." Then I compare them with the homes for sale by realtors. I check *The Vancouver Sun*, *The Province*, and sometimes *The Surrey Leader.* If a property sounds interesting, I get on the phone. If what I learn from the phone conversation interests me, I get into my car and take a look at the property. I have a quick look and come back.

> *"Genius and success are 90% hard work, but only 10% brilliant, original concepts."*
>
> *(Thomas Edison)*

I don't know exactly how much time I spend a week at all this, but it's a lot. It's like a second full time job.

Is there anything in these newspaper ads which makes you take more interest in one over another?

Well, sometimes the owner says that the price is "firm." This is a good sign because it usually means that I'm not going to waste a lot of time haggling over the price. Chances are that the place is priced right in the first instance. The vendor is serious about selling and not just testing the market to see if s/he can find any suckers around. On the other hand, I have seen lots of "for sale by owner" houses which were terribly overpriced.

Are there any other ways to find good deals?

I keep my eyes open when I'm driving around. Sometimes a "for sale" sign in front of a house will catch my eye. I might make a note of who has the listing and give them a call. This is how I found the house on 80th Ave. (house No. 3).

I also go to open houses. These give me lots of ideas about prices, what's available, and even decorating ideas. I use these ideas to improve all of my properties. Two years ago, for instance, I bought an apartment in the West End of Vancouver and I was able to apply some of these decorating ideas and increase the value of this unit dramatically. More about that later.

Recently I have being going further afield (Cloverdale, Langley) and I'm now looking into acreage. This is where I hope to really strike it rich. I haven't tapped this part of the market yet, but I will.

What does real estate mean to you? What does it do for you?

It's a great challenge to me and it feels so great when I make a good deal. The contest of wills. Interpreting a vendor's motivation. I feel that I have been right in most of my decisions and with each successful decision my confidence has increased. So has my respect for myself, which is so precious to me.

I also love making money and I love the way money opens doors for you in life. Okay, I guess you can say that I'm addicted, but not to the point of madness. There are worse addictions, aren't there? I could be hooked on gambling and take big risks with my hard-earned money.

Let's summarize, shall we? Let's go back to April, 1992. What properties do you own and what are your next moves?

I own four houses and two apartments (condos):

THE HOUSES	THE APARTMENTS
• House 2 (77A Ave.)	• Condo 1 (137th St., Carriage Lane)
• House 3 (80th Ave.)	• Condo 2 (137th St., Carriage Lane)
• House 5 (70th Ave.)	
• House 6 (97th Ave.)	

54

Here's a summary by photos:

HOUSES	HOUSES	CONDOS
No. 1 (sold)	No. 4 (sold)	No. 1
No. 2	No. 5	No. 2
No. 3	No. 6	

If it's April 1992, my next move is to buy an apartment in the West End of Vancouver at 1146 Harwood St.

Physical details about Condo No. 3:

> — a "studio" or "bachelor" (520 square feet) apartment but a large Murphy bed (tips up to become part of the wall) made it seem bigger
> — well-kept, clean, strata title highrise building
> — in the lively, densely populated "West End" of Vancouver
> — only two blocks from the Stanley Park Seawall
> — on second floor, facing south (a big plus!) onto gardens
— bathroom with a jacuzzi
> — freshly painted, required no repairs
> — mirrored wall (floor to ceiling) gives impression of space
> — stackable ensuite washer and dryer
> — a small dishwasher in the kitchen

The West End of Vancouver, 1146 Harwood St.
Aqlim's suite is on the left side of the building.

Financial summary of Condo No. 3:

— Asking price:	$118,000
— What Aqlim paid:	$106,000
— Down payment:	$0
— Mortgage:	+ $106,000
— Total:	$106,000
— Apartment rents for:	$950
— monthly mort. payment:	− $980
— Net loss:	$30

**Your description of this apartment is quite detailed.
Maybe even more detailed than your descriptions
of your houses. Why are you going into such detail?**

Because when it comes to flipping, the details for apartments are more critical. Your margin of profit is less. So is your margin of error. If you buy a house well below market value (let's say, 15% below), the house usually will sell itself. Apartments are different. Even if you find one for 15% below market value, you might not find it as easy to sell. It has to have lots of good features. And no really bad features. For instance, condos which face north are much harder to sell (at least in Vancouver). Because of the crime rate, ground floor units are not easy to flip.

> **"What counts in real estate is location, location, and location."**
> *(A realtor's saying)*

The apartment we are talking about (1146 Harwood) had lots of good features and I knew that it would not be hard to flip at a profit. It had good location, which is the single most important thing to consider. It had a garden and ocean view. The building was well looked after. The jacuzzi was appealing (very fashionable these days). Because of the mirrored wall and the Murphy bed the place seemed much larger than it was. Impressions sell. I think that these are the main things to look for when you buy an apartment.

My game-plan was to flip this unit when the right moment came, but in the meantime to furnish it and rent it out for whatever the market would bear. I had heard that I could get about $1,000 a month for a nicely furnished apartment and I was eager to put this rumour to the test.

I found that furnishings are not expensive if you shop around. In my driving around I discovered a furniture discount place on 72nd Ave. and 134th St. in Surrey. It's called J. R. Furniture. They buy up furniture from bankruptcies and then sell the stuff at a big discount. Excellent deals:

— a dining room set (brass and glass table with
  elegant dusty rose upholstery): $115

View south from the condo at 1146 Harwood St. A communal garden directly below, the sea in the distance.

— a black and rose sofa:	$500
— an armchair:	$100

I shopped around for whatever else I needed to make this apartment appeal to the 'classier' kind of tenant e. g., a business person visiting Vancouver or maybe a yuppie of some kind:

— a 20 inch colour T. V. (with remote) from Future Shop:	$250
— a VCR from Costco (people are much more likely to rent your furnished place if you have a VCR. I'd say it's more a necessity than a luxury):	$200
— dishes, cutlery and bedding amounted to very little:	$300
Total of:	$1465

For a pretty modest sum ($1,500) I was ready to rent out a tastefully decorated, completely furnished apartment. My plan was to rent it out for $1,000 a month, which would just about take care of the mortgage and the mortgage on this unit was pretty high: 100%! In other words, I bought the place with no money down.

Aw, come on, Aqlim. Who are you kidding? That's Tom Vu stuff!

Let me explain the total picture. The vendor had been asking $118,000 but I knew from the realtor that she was desperate to sell so I put in a low offer ($106,000). I didn't think she would bite at such a low offer, but she did.

Anyway, she accepted it without even trying to bargain the price up. I would have been prepared to pay at least a few thousand dollars more (say $108,000) but I'm certainly not going to offer to do this! I honestly can't understand her quickness to accept $106,000 but there's lots about people which is beyond understanding. At least I find it so, and it's just as well to keep this in mind when dealing in real estate. *It pays sometimes to make a low offer. You never know: they just might accept! Why worry about the vendor being insulted?*

Is there any pattern that you follow in bargaining?

More or less, yes. I carefully determine what my offer will be, and it's always low. They might counter to meet me part way. If they don't, I lose interest in the property. If they do come down, I might make one counter offer to this price. Only one. No more. If they don't accept it, I'm in my car and off.

But what's this about buying condo 3 with no money down?

That's exactly what I did. I didn't have any readily available cash for the down payment ($25,000). So I enquired about buying it with no money down. The realtor who showed me the place, Cam Foster, had some creative ideas on financing and the contacts to implement these ideas. By the way, up to this point I had thought that buying with no money down was something that you could only do in the U.S.A. (maybe in fantasy on the Tom Vu show), but not in the highly regulated society of Canada. I was wrong and had to change my thinking.

Cam made some enquiries for me. It turned out that Vancity was prepared to offer me a mortgage for the total amount of the Harwood St. apartment: $106,000. I learned that this kind of mortgage is called "inter-alia." I didn't care what it was called as long as it got me the money which I needed to buy this apartment. By this time I really wanted to prove that one could buy a place with no money down.

After I made a few enquiries, I was even more certain that I couldn't help but make money on this apartment. I asked Cam to run a computer check on recent past sales in the building (1146 Harwood) and it was clear from these figures that my second floor unit was underpriced at $106,000.

I also got your opinion since you live in the West End, do some speculation there yourself and know the prices very well. Everything suggested that I was going to make money on it.

Yes, I thought you couldn't miss. How does an inter-alia mortgage work?

You have to already own equity in some kind of property. What the bank or Vancity (or whoever) does, is use as 'collateral' the equity that you have in your own residence (in my case this amounts to about $150,000). If I happen to sell my residence, then I am obliged to pay a certain sum towards the inter-alia mortgage.

However, this is not a problem because I am not planning to sell my residence although I did have it on the market recently (just testing the water . . .). Mind you, I listed my home at a very hefty price and if I had got close to what I was asking, it would have been "an offer you can't refuse" and I gladly would have put up with the hassle of moving if I'd been able to clear over $100,000.

To get back to the great deal which you got on the furniture, how did you do this? I saw that dining room set and can't believe how little you paid for it. I paid twice as much for an identical used one through the want ads! Are you lucky, or what?

I really don't think so. Maybe we can say that I make luck happen by taking time to shop and look into things. I do a lot of driving around and that is how I found out about J. R. Furniture. It sounds like I was just lucky, but I spend a lot of time driving around checking out prices. This takes a lot of time and effort. I can't overstate the importance of this. If anyone thinks it's easy, it's because they forget about all the time that I spend at this kind of thing.

The point is that I do it so much that it has become a habit. However, it seems to be a habit that not that many people are prepared to bother to acquire. It's the same kind of thing with furniture (or stamps, coins or antiques) as it is with houses and property. *It takes a lot of time and effort to learn how to recognize a good deal.*

Sometimes when I drive around, I stumble on something really good. When I do, I take advantage of it. In this case I asked the liquidators for their business card so that I could get in touch with them again if I needed new furniture cheap. It's all part of my networking. *I have built up a good network in a lot of areas: where to get the cheapest mortgage, where to get the cheapest furniture, how to find the cheapest real estate deals, etc.*

Getting back to renting out furnished apartments, your other two units (Carriage Lane in Surrey) were rented out unfurnished. Now that you've rented out a furnished unit as well, do you think it was a good idea? Would you do it again?

I'd be reluctant to get involved with a similar arrangement because the West End is too far from my home in Surrey. And there are other disadvantages. When you rent out furnished dwellings you are responsible to make sure that everything is in good working order. If the TV goes on the blink, you have to deal with it, immediately. This happened at 1146 Harwood. The TV did go on the blink. There could be all kinds of emergencies: hot water tank, broken garburator, etc.

You also have to consider that the kind of person who wants furnished accommodation often doesn't want it for very long. Maybe a month or so. So you have to keep advertising. $80 or so every time you want to run an ad in *The Vancouver Sun* or *The Province* (which, by the way, is where you're going to find your best tenants, business people and the like). Maybe a film worker from Toronto who's in Vancouver for a month or so while his company is shooting a movie.

If people don't stay long, then you have to keep advertising. You have to keep driving the 25 miles from Surrey to show the apartment, and maybe to someone who isn't going to take it. You have to drive in and clean up every time someone vacates the apartment. You probably have to hire a carpet cleaner every time there is a new tenant. It was too much of a hassle.

On the other hand, my overall plan worked very well. I owned 1146 Harwood for only a year and it brought in $950 a month rent. This rent took care of almost all the mortgage. All this suited me just fine because my main objective had been to flip and make money and this is exactly what I did. Also, by venturing into the area of apartments (and the West End) I had the satisfaction of taking a bit of a risk and coming out smiling. Each time I try some thing new like this I come out feeling stronger and more confident.

"Gingerbread sells."

(A realtors' saying)

I sold 1146 Harwood for $122,000 (March 1993), so after I negotiated what I thought was a fair commission ($6,000) I walked away with about $10,000 profit:

— Bought unit for:	$106,000
— sold it for:	$122,000
— realtor's commission:	$6,000
— profit (approx.):	$10,000

By the way, your realtor may consider a reduced commission if he is "double-ending" the property, which means that he gets a commission for listing the property and a commission for selling it. This is what happened at 1146 Harwood. When you make a deal with a realtor you should always write this clause into the listing agreement, or have it clearly understood between you and the realtor if you have so much trust between you that you feel comfortable with verbal agreements.

Okay. You've sold your apartment in the West End and made $10,000. What was your next move?

I bought another condo in Surrey. A very large two-bedroom in a complex called Park Woods. The vendors were asking only $109,000. Dick Balchen tipped me off that this two-bedroom condo was considerably underpriced. I thought that I'd test the water with $100,000 just to see what would happen. To my delight they accepted the offer and $100,000 is all that I paid for it. They could have bargained with me and I would have come up, but for some strange reason they didn't (were they getting jittery about losing my offer?). Well, whatever! I'm not going to argue with that!

What prompted you to think that $100,000 was a good price to pay? Had you done any research?

Yes, I knew a couple of very useful things. I knew that the two Surrey apartments which I owned in Carriage Lane (condo Nos. 1 and 2) had gone up in price by about $20,000 each since I bought them and I felt that Park Woods was comparable to Carriage Lane.

Carriage Lane seemed like a good comparable and from that point of view $100,000 was a good price. Here's a photo of the Park Woods complex:

Park Woods Complex. Note the feeling of space in the communal area.

Then there was another piece of useful information. I knew from the listing realtor that the vendors had already bought another place and that they had to sell the two-bedroom quickly in order to remove the "subject to" clause on their new offer. They were pretty close to desperate and I knew that they would look at almost any offer. April 30, 1993 was their closing date so they had to sell the two-bedroom by that date. They had only about a week.

Anyway, they accepted my offer. I guess the moral of this tale is that *you shouldn't think about buying any property until you have sold what you already own.* Even if it means renting for a while, putting some stuff in storage, or whatever. Sell one unit, then look for another. Unless, of course, you have access to lots of cash. If you don't follow this rule you put yourself at the mercy of the market and risk not getting any good offers. The market is something you can never be sure of second-guessing.

"A fool and his gold are soon parted."
(ancient proverb)

The other rule which I think is important is this: *ask your realtor to contact you as soon as s/he comes across one of the scenarios mentioned on page 24.* These are often the best deals. Realtors often know a lot about vendors' financial circumstances and may be able to give you sound advice based on their knowledge. If circumspect, they can do this without compromising their obligation to respect the vendor's privacy.

One thing is certain: if you phone a realtor at random and say that you want to look at property, you can be sure that the realtor is going to show you a lot a property which isn't underpriced at all. Why waste your time looking at such property? Have your realtor inform you only about the *good* deals, housing on which the asking price is already low or can probably be substantially reduced. Of course you have to keep doing your homework yourself so that you'll be able to know good deals when you see them.

What is this two-bedroom unit like?

Physical details about condo No. 4:

- — 1025 square feet (bigger than my house No. 5!)
- — strata title (so you own your share of the land it's on)
- — 2 bedrooms; only one bathroom
- — dishwasher, gas fireplace
- — underground parking and storage

— complex has an exercise room, sauna, jacuzzi, squash court

You can see my unit at the top left of this photograph:

CONDO NO. 4
13480 96th Ave.

Financial summary of condo No. 4:

— Asking price:	$109,000
— What Aqlim paid:	$100,000
— Down payment:	$10,000
— Mortgage:	$90,000
— Total:	$100,000
— Condo rents out for:	$750
— Monthly mort. payment:	$690
— Net gain per month:	$60

So I paid 10% down and took out a mortgage for $90,000 at 7.25%, which amounts to payments of $690 per month. I am renting it out for $750 per month so this property is almost paying for itself. Stewing in its own juice, like all my units. The tenants have signed a year's lease, which I recommend. There is a monthly maintenance fee of $150 (which I have left out of this financial summary in order to keep things clear and simple) so the bottom line is that I pay $50 a month to keep this place simmering on the great stove of real estate.

The tenant is an elderly man who has a wife and a teenage daughter. They seem to be stable and reliable so my mind is at rest. Also, they like the place so much that they are making overtures about renting with an option to buy. I'll have to look into this before I decide what I am going to do.

What are your plans for this apartment?

It has already increased in value and I bought it only a few weeks ago. *I know that it has appreciated because I tested the market by advertising it in the paper for $114,000, partly to see what would happen.* No sooner had the ad appeared than I received an offer from someone who wanted to rent it with an option to buy it eventually at full price. However, by the terms of their offer I would have received only $5,000 as a down payment.

I refused this offer because I knew that the apartment must be worth more. It *had* to be worth more if there was such a fast offer for the full price as soon as the ad came out. *It's not a bad idea to run an ad just to test the market and confirm to yourself the value of your property.*

Would it be a good idea to rent out the place with an option to buy, or not? How do you arrange this?

I wasn't really interested in the arrangement, so I didn't pursue it. I did talk to a lawyer, and he told me that if I wanted a rent-with-option-to- buy arrangement I should have him draft up an agreement. According to the agreement the tenants would have to come up with at least 10% down and borrow enough money to pay off the balance of the place within a year. But I want money now, not later, so an arrangement like this doesn't interest me.

In any case, I think that the value of this property will go up, so I am going to hang onto it for at least a year. The apartment is close to the big Surrey Place Shopping Mall. And the new Sky Train station. For Surrey, it's got a great central location. It's got to go up.

Okay. You own four houses plus three condos. Where do you go from here?

I intend to stay in the game. I have another house in mind at this moment. A neighbour of mine has a house on the market for $167,000 but I am almost sure that he will accept $157,000. He has it rented out right now for $950 a month and I'm pretty sure that I can rent it out for the same amount. So here is another unit that will pay for itself and increase in value as property values in general increase (which I feel they will).

A lot of people all over the world find (Greater) Vancouver's image appealing and I think that they'll keep on coming here to settle. And Surrey is looking better all the time as it acquires newer and better housing (see p. 29), more sophisticated amenities like Guildford Mall, The Surrey Arts Center, the Sky Train, various new libraries, elegant restaurants (like La Masia, the Black Forest, Blooms, Hazlemere Golf and Country Club) and so on.

Does this mean that for your next deal you're going with a house rather than an apartment?

Yes, I prefer houses to condos because houses tend to increase in value more. Houses are on their own land and there is something very attractive about that. Condos might hold their value but they don't increase in value fast enough. Okay, they *are* safer than houses but you can't often make big money in a hurry on them.

Are you tempted to sell any of the properties which you own at this moment?

No, I'm going to sit tight and I'm not going to part with anything for a while. Everything is going my way for the moment so I'm not going to rock the boat. I like the idea of hanging on to some of this property for when I get old. With the income that they generate, they will make life a lot easier.

After all your mortgage payments and other financial commitments do you find that you have much disposable income at the end of each month?

Disposable what ?! No, I have very little of *that* at the end of each month. My budget is very, very tight.

Are you pleased with that state of affairs?

My needs are met but I do adhere to a tight budget. Basically I allow only for my needs and those of my son. However, if I'm short, I can always go to the bank and borrow some. It's also nice to know that I could raise a large sum very quickly by selling any one of my units. I bought all of them for less than market value and it would be easy to sell any of them.

But I'm quite happy with the way things are. Real estate challenges me, and so for that matter does the necessity of following a pretty strict budget. I think it's healthy to feel challenged to a certain point.

You've just said, "I don't have any savings." Could you comment on this?

I don't have any savings to speak of, but it's not entirely by choice. To some degree it's just the way things happen. For instance, last year I had to pay a $7,000 penalty for cancelling the mortgage on my principal residence and taking out a new mortgage with another bank. The rate which I had been paying was horrible: 11% (for five years) so it was well worthwhile to pay the penalty fee of $7,000 just to get out from under it.

The shift was from the Scotiabank to the Canadian Imperial Bank of Commerce. I first got the idea when a friend, a businessman, suggested it. When the interest rates dropped in 1992 to about 7.5% it seemed like a very good way to save a lot of money. It's funny what you discover when you start talking to people and crunching numbers. In this case I discovered that the $7,000 penalty which I had dreaded was nothing compared with the money that I'd be saving in the long run by refinancing. And, by the way, my new mortgage is based on prime variable.

According to my calculations, I will save approximately $7,000 a year for the next five years because of the reduced mortgage rate which I now have. This is a saving of $28,000. Not bad, I think.

You put me in mind of the old British saying, "Penny wise, pound foolish." It seems to me that in taking a step like transferring your mortgage you are saving megabucks in the long run. You are certainly not "pound foolish" here!

Yes, your attitude has a lot to do with whether or not you'll see far enough past your fear and unreasonable caution in order to see the new possibilities which lie just around the corner and can only be seen if you are aggressive enough to look at things in a broader way. In this case I took the time to crunch the numbers and realized that paying out $7,000 was nothing compared with saving $28,000 over the next five years ($35,000 - $7,000 = $28,000).

72,792 people moved to British Columbia last year (1994). 38,649 came from other parts of Canada.

Anyway, to get back to your question: no, I find it very hard to keep much money in savings. For one thing, whatever I have in this kind of reserve seems to constantly get eaten up by unforeseeable expenses: $7,000 extra out of the blue to pay Revenue Canada (for taxable capital gains) this year. $5,000 to buy out the Beretta which I've been leasing for the past few years. $7,000 to the Scotiabank for the mortgage penalty. On and on it goes. That's where all the savings go!

Besides, I don't think it's very smart to put much money into savings because the interest rate is a pitiful 4% or so. (At the moment I have only $6,000 in the bank.) In the overall picture I have no regrets whatsoever about having most of my money tied up in property because I know that I can count on my investment property to pay off much more handsomely in the long run. Property in the Lower Mainland will keep going up. And, as I said, I can always get a loan from the bank if I need money. They don't have any problem lending to someone like me!

You mentioned capital gains tax. A dreaded phrase for many people. Does capital gains tax worry you and make you cautious?

No way. I look at it this way. I pay what I have to and I don't mind the thought that my taxes will help society in general. Let's say that I make $10,000 on a flip (as I did with condo No. 3) and have to pay 30% capital gains tax on this profit because it is profit which I made on a rental property (this is tax which I wouldn't have to pay if it were a question of my principal residence). I don't see this tax as a big deal compared with the $7,000 I will clear on the transaction. I prefer to act (buy) and accentuate the positive rather than do nothing and moan about the tax. (*Editor's note, 1995: the 30% above would now be 37%.*)

On the subject of taxes I should mention a tax break which I've discovered. One is to buy a condo in a relative's name. For instance, I bought condo No. 2 in my son's name and co-signed the mortgage for him. Since he is in a very low income bracket there will be next to nothing to pay in capital gains tax when we sell this unit.

You seem to be at home wheeling and dealing. Do you think that this is result of your character or is it the influence that your upbringing in Pakistan had on you?

A bit of both, I think. In Pakistan there are far fewer laws and restrictions. Mortgages exist but most transactions are done in cash. Capital gains do not exist. Income tax exists, but it is very easy to avoid paying any.

Because of the freedom it offers, Pakistan encourages you to think in a sly, even somewhat selfish way. Everyone becomes an expert at twisting the law around. Living in Pakistan also encourages confidence. The people who have money become very confident and bold in their investment habits. I find it very different in Canada where the laws are very strict and I think that it is this strictness which causes many Canadians to be cautious, even fearful about speculative investment. Although, when you put your mind to it, you can find ways to soften this strictness, even here.

I grew up with the idea that investing in property is uncomplicated and easy (as long as you have the money in the first place!) In my family the prevailing attitude was like the T-shirt slogan: "Just do it!" I was lucky that father was quite well off. I watched him buy at least a dozen properties. Who knows? Maybe such an example of boldness left its mark on me.

It seems to me that you are playing real life Monopoly very well, Aqlim. How would you say the game has affected you? Has it changed your life?

Let me tell you something. Buying and selling real estate has given me a sense of security and a feeling of confidence. I was certainly very frightened when I bought my first and second houses but with each subsequent

72

purchase I have acquired confidence. This constantly-increasing confidence has given me the boldness required to find out how the real estate game works and to buy property which I never would have even considered buying before that change in my character.

I certainly didn't have self-confidence when I was living in an apartment. At the present time I also feel more respected, not because I have the answers, but because of the efforts I have made.

These feelings of mine are often reinforced by other people, which is great. I get lots of compliments from my friends. I also get compliments from people whom I hardly know, which delights me. The other day in the Xerox room at school one of the teachers asked me how my "real estate business" was going. I had to laugh because this teacher doesn't even know me. It turns out that he had heard things through the grapevine. I had to laugh. I was flattered.

Then, naturally, there are the financial rewards which I commented on at the beginning of this interview. A beautiful house. An attractive car. Lots of travel. Enough money for me to keep regularly in touch with my large and much loved family (most of whom live in Pakistan and the U.K.). Yes, my life has been radically changed, and for the better.

SUMMARY OF TRANSACTIONS

Unit	Bought for	Date	Sold When	Price	Est. Mark Val	Profit	Own.
H#1 (66A)	$79K	'84	'88	$93K	$195K	$14K	
H#2 77A	$103K	'87	-	-	$250K	$147K (Theo)	
H#3 80	$75K	'89	-	-	$160K	$85K (Theo.)	
H#4 66A	$78K	'89	'91	$135K	$165K	$57K	(1/2) P
H#5 70	$118K	'90			$165K	$47K	(1/2) P
C#1 100	$72.9K	'91			$95K	$22K (Theo.)	
C#2 100	$76K	'91			$98K	$22K (Theo.)	
H#6 97	$145.	'92			$185K	$40K (Theo.)	
C#3 Harw.	$106K	'91	'92		$122K	$16K	
C#4 96	$100K	'93			$120K	$20K (Theo.)	
						$400,000	

Aqlim's total theoretical profit as of July, 1993 is $400,000. If you add to this figure her total equity in all 8 units the total is close to $500,000. What's next? Who knows? Aqlim is looking into acreage further up the Fraser Valley.

Total as of July, 1993: Aqlim owns 4 houses with an estimated total market value of $760,000.

She also owns 3 condos with an estimated value of $315,000. This amounts to a total of $1,075,000. If you subtract the total of what she owes on the various mortgages ($500,000) and subtract this amount from the total market value of the units, you get a rough idea of how much money she is worth: $575,000.

What with increasing property values and renters paying off her mortgages, she'll be a millionaire before long.

Market value of all units:	$1,075,000
Total of mortgages owing:	− $500,000
Estimated net worth:	$575,000

Summary by photos

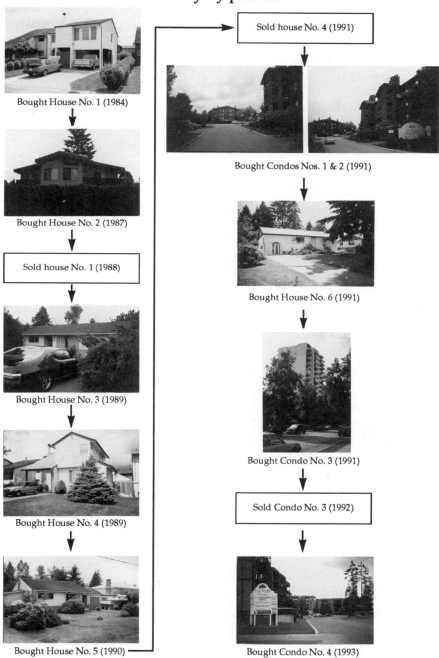

Bought House No. 1 (1984)

Bought House No. 2 (1987)

Sold house No. 1 (1988)

Bought House No. 3 (1989)

Bought House No. 4 (1989)

Bought House No. 5 (1990)

Sold house No. 4 (1991)

Bought Condos Nos. 1 & 2 (1991)

Bought House No. 6 (1991)

Bought Condo No. 3 (1991)

Sold Condo No. 3 (1992)

Bought Condo No. 4 (1993)

Editor's Note:

Since *Hot Tips* first appeared in December 1993, Aqlim has bought two more houses and unloaded one of her condos. As usual, she has picked up some hot new tips to pass on to you!

Tell us about the first house you bought in early 1994. How did you find it? What made you think that it was a good deal?

It's curious how it happened. I was driving along one day and, as usual, keeping my eyes open. (Okay, I was thinking about real estate! You *know* it!) Something peculiar caught my eye. On the lawn of a house there were two "for sale" signs. What was odd is that each sign listed a different company and a different realtor.

I phoned my realtor and found out that there was a divorce in the picture (see p. 24). A couple was not getting along and they had put the house on the market at $179,000. I was taken with this house right away. It had a pleasant, woodsy location and the basement could easily be converted to a rentable suite.

To determine my *starting offer* I gathered information. The bank's appraisal ($170,000) suggested that the asking price was not out of line and the computer comparables confirmed my impression.

Still, thinking that this couple would be in a hurry to sell, I made them a very lowball offer of $140,000. They countered me with $160,000 and I re-countered this with an offer of $145,000. No bites, so I increased the offer to $150,000. The couple countered with $159,000. I didn't quibble with this figure because it was still a good deal and I knew that if I didn't take it very soon, someone else would. The house has to be worth $185,000 at least.

Looks to me like your negotiations are becoming bolder. More complex. More sophisticated. Doesn't it take a lot of nerve to counter $179,000 with $140,000?

I suppose that it does. It doesn't faze me one bit if they find $140,000 insulting. There are lots of good deals out there and sooner or later someone will accept my offer.

But, you know, it is actually to my advantage to take my time and make several counter-offers, as I did in this case. By taking my time and letting out just a little fishing line at a time I am strengthening my bargaining position. Both the vendor and the real estate agents will interpret my actions as a sign that I am not particularly eager. This is exactly what I want them to think so that they will fear losing me altogether and will therefore stay in the ball game. Besides, even a low offer doesn't look despicable if there are no others.

House No. 7.
Photo at left is taken
from the back lawn,
at the bottom of
which is a wild
ravine,
Bear Creek —
very woodsy.
(140th St., Surrey).

Anything else we should know about this house?

Yes, I'm renting it out for $1,000 a month and this covers the mortgage. Also, although this property is not zoned as "multi-family dwelling" now, I noticed that there are townhouses only a few blocks away so I think it quite possible that sooner or later the zoning could change and I could put up a duplex or a triplex.

The lot is big – 86 feet wide by 143 feet deep. It has three bedrooms. The basement could be made into a rentable suite. And, best of all, I paid the $5,000 down payment with my Visa! The mortgage is large, but it's being covered by the rent.

Oh, I forgot to mention: this is the first house that I hired a house inspector to look at.

Is that a worthwhile thing to do?

Absolutely! An inspector is an expert at spotting problems which most people wouldn't notice: plumbing and wiring problems, dry rot, termites, a roof that needs replacing, problems with the foundation and structure, etc. It's a bit like buying a used car and having it inspected by an expert mechanic at the B.C. Automobile Association. Sure, it costs $90 or whatever, but you will at least know whether or not you're getting saddled with a lemon. You are getting objective advice from an expert who has no axe to grind.

How much does an inspection cost?

About $250 – and make sure that whoever you hire is certified. (Look in the *Yellow Pages* under "Building Inspectors.") My inspector gave my 'new' house high marks, which did a lot to put my mind at rest. Who needs more stress?

Yes, I've quite enough of that, thank you very much! If the inspector had found defects in the house, how would this have affected you?

That all depends on how many and how bad. If he'd found some major things wrong (and a new roof can easily cost $7,000) I would have got estimates on how much it would cost to fix them then I would have used this information to obtain a further price reduction. Or I would have used the negative report to back out of the deal, period. Get my deposit back and run!

Don't you risk scaring off the seller if you insist on having the house inspected and make this one of the 'subject to' clauses in your written offer?

I don't think so. A vendor would have to be very crazy to take offense at a reasonable request for an inspection.

How useful to the buyer is the Property Condition Disclosure Statement that the B.C. government has cooked up (September 1993)? Can't the buyer insist on the vendor filling out one of these forms?

Sure, but what does this "statement" mean? Even if the vendor doesn't exactly lie about things, there's lots that s/he can't see.

The kind of inspection that you paid for personally is a bit of an extra, isn't it? I mean, you bought information which was valuable to you personally. Didn't you have to pay for another inspection as well – the one that the bank or other mortgage institution insists that the purchaser have carried out?

Yes, you're right, but the bank's inspection is called an *appraisal,* and it doesn't go into structural defects and things like that very much. Its purpose is only to determine what the house is worth. These bank appraisals are a big pain in the neck but banks insist on them so they're unavoidable. The only thing you *can* do is cut corners on their fees, and this is what did when I bought my next house (#8), but I'll tell you about that later. Be sure to ask for a copy of the appraisal – you paid for it.

What was your next move, Aqlim?

I decided to incorporate under the name "Barlas Investments Inc." By doing this I will substantially reduce my income tax. It's easy math: I pay 40% tax as a private individual; as a corporation I pay 25%. This is an enormous saving and it's legal. And incorporation is simple: I had my lawyer do it. Total cost: $900.

However, I have decided that it's well worthwhile to hire a lawyer whenever you buy or sell (in spite of what I said about notaries on p. 41). A good lawyer will spot problems that a notary might miss. At least that's my opinion now.

> *"To do well in real estate you need an energetic realtor, a flexible banker and an astute lawyer."*
>
> **(a common saying in real estate)**

I nearly forgot to ask: do you insure your properties?

Always! And against every possible disaster, including earthquakes. I do the same for personal possessions.

I understand that you sold one of your condos about this time.

Yes, I sold condo #2 [see p. 48] in Carriage Lane for $90,000. The tenants were being difficult and that unit was never going to appreciate much. I had thought that the completion of the new Skytrain stations would have driven values up but this didn't happen. Also, I hadn't foreseen that there would be a big glut of condos landing on the market this year and that this would drive prices down. Shows you that you can't predict the future!

I bailed out of that same development. Just about broke even, I think.

Yes, well, I came away from that experience determined

to stick with houses and I soon bought another house in the Tynehead area of Surrey (see map on p. 28 – Tynehead is between Newton and Cloverdale). I'm staying clear of condos from now on.

Tynehead is scaling itself up, as you can see from the following photograph.

There's a lot of new houses and townhouses being built in this area and this flurry of building will eventually push up the value of my place.

When I first looked at the place I bought [house #8], it seemed very old [it's actually 35] and run-down, but the lot was huge, 87 by 92 feet, and I realized that I shouldn't let myself be put off by appearances. The property alone had to be worth $160,000, and I was determined to keep this in mind while mulling over what kind of offer to make. Besides, I remember reading somewhere that it's often wise to buy the most run-down place on a good street, which I think is good advice.

How did the negotiations go?

Complicated and a bit strange but I learned from them. The vendors were asking $165,000. I had my realtor

House #8, in the Tynehead area of Surrey.

check the comparables and found that this price was reasonable. I offered $130,000; they countered with $149,000. Then I heard from my realtor that someone had offered $145,000 and the owners were furious and insulted, and had rejected the offer. I knew that I had to act fast and come in higher. So I offered $148,000 and it was accepted.

What I learned from these transactions is that extreme anger can be a very revealing thing, in this case a sign that the house really was underpriced at $149,000 and that I was getting a bargain.

Excellent! Reminds me of the scene towards the end of *Macbeth* where Malcolm falsely makes himself out to be a rat in order to test Macduff's sincerity. And when Macduff flies into a rage Malcolm can see how sincere Macduff is. Isn't it amazing what you can learn from the classics?

It is. When I went to the bank for a mortgage, the Scotiabank wanted to charge me $200 for an appraisal. I told them that I had paid only $80 to the CIBC for a similar service [house #7] so the Scotiabank matched the lower price. If you don't ask, you don't get! And this strategy applies to any of those ugly fees which lending institutions hit you with: renewal fees, discharge fees. You can often have both of these waived.

Is there anything else you'd like to say about the transaction of house 8?

Not much. The mortgage payments are $918 and the present rent is only $650 a month so I'll have to raise it unless I can make a deal with the tenant so that she does some painting and maintenance work for me in return for reduced rent. I did learn something useful about having a good lawyer through this transaction. Let me tell you about it.

It seems there was a city covenant on house #8 and according to this covenant the Municipality of Surrey wanted the owner to remove a septic tank immediately. The owner didn't seem about to do this and certainly hadn't written it down in the Disclosure Statement. Fortunately, my lawyer picked up on this and withheld $5,000 of my money. He will continue to withhold it until the vendor removes the septic tank. I don't think that anyone but a good lawyer would have spotted this wrinkle. You get what you pay for.

So since January 1994 you bought two houses and sold one condo.

Yes, I've been working hard, but I've made three good moves. Both houses were underpriced, especially house #7. And both are located in desirable areas and will be easy to rent out. Again, the rents will more or less pay off the mortgages and in the long run the price of housing will continue to climb.

This is especially true for lower-priced housing, which is what I tend to buy. Prices are more volatile at the top end of the market so you have to be more careful if that's where you're putting your money. At the top end you stand to make more, and to lose more . . .

Also, I am so very pleased to get rid of that condo! I

made only a few thousand on it, and it was foolish to tie up capital in a unit that wasn't making much money.

What are your plans for the future, Aqlim?

Oh, I'll keep on investing. I'm hooked and I love it. Acreage is next, and I've already started looking into it. Please relay my thanks to our readers for their supportive mail. It has meant a lot to me.

HOT TIPS FROM THOMSON'S NETWORK OF EXPERTS

Since the first appearance of HOT TIPS FOR REAL ESTATE INVESTORS (December, 1993) I have had a chance to talk with many realtors, mortgage brokers, investors and readers of HOT TIPS. These conversations have prompted many useful changes throughout the original HOT TIPS.

They have also made me aware that several questions need to be answered in greater detail: How do you raise money? (Especially young people: how do they raise money?) Where should you buy? How do you evaluate prospective tenants? What are the crucial steps to take in order to get a great deal on your first place? What should you read in order to understand the market?

I picked quite a few brains (there are some very generous people out there . . .) and I have included my findings in this second edition. I take sole responsibility for these ideas.

— Robert Stuart Thomson,
Co-author of HOT TIPS and editor of Godwin Books.

These ideas have been grouped into seven sections:

I. EIGHT WAYS TO RAISE MONEY FOR THAT "STEAL OF A DEAL."

(Important hints, especially for the younger generation who have had bad luck demographically.)

Below you will find listed a number of ways to raise serious money towards a purchase. For brevity's sake I have explained just enough for you to know if you want to look further into the idea. If you do, consult your realtor/mortgage broker/bank manager (for starters, anyway), and/or phone one of the excellent contacts who are listed at the end of this book.

1. REVERSE MORTGAGES, a.k.a. home equity conversion programs. Parents who have lots of equity in their own home can obtain a lump sum from this equity and use this money as a loan/gift for their children's down payment and/or mortgage. A neat way to help a young person get started in real estate! Good jobs for young people are scarce and real estate prices inevitably climb so the sooner young people get started, the better! Seven points about reverse mortgages:

a.   For property owners over 60.
b.   Unlocks 12-36% of your equity.
c.   Money unlocked is tax-free.
d.   You continue to own your own home.
e.   No monthly payments (the mortgage company is repaid when your estate is settled).
f.   If your property value increases, so does your residual equity. Even if property prices collapse you can never owe more than the value of your home.
g.   You are not tied down; you can still sell and move.

This program might not be available in all parts of Canada but you can check it out (and get other information) by phoning or writing:

```
1-800- 563-2447
Canadian Home Income Plan,
#2570, 1066 W. Hastings St.
Vancouver, V6E 3X1

(Also available through the Toronto-Dominion Bank)
```

2. FIRST TIME BUYERS
(and this can include divorcees).

Use the Canada Mortgage and Housing Corporation's (CMHC's) "5% down" program. By (Canadian) law, lending institutions can lend you a maximum of 75% of the property price. Fortunately, with the CMHC program they will allow you to borrow up to 95%, which means that as a first time buyer you have to come up with only 5% of the purchase price as a down payment.

For this convenient service CMHC charges a fee of 2 1/2% of the mortgage value plus a $75 application fee. On a $200,000 mortgage this equates to $5,000. (In this case they'd add the $5,000 to your mortgage, making a total of $205,000 on which your interest payments must be made.) The "5% down" program has enabled thousands of Canadians to finance their first home.

In the Lower Mainland the ceiling on a qualifying mortgage is currently (October, 1995) $250,000 but this could change. Also, the actual premium you pay varies with the loan to value ratio. See a CMHC representative for details. The conditions of their 5% down program tend to change, so it is best to phone them for up-to-date information (in Vancouver: 604-731-5733). Their free booklet is also useful.

RRSP'S. If you have money sitting in your RRSP you can use up to $20,000 ($40,000 per couple) of it for your down payment. There is one catch: this money has to be paid back to your RRSP within 15 years with minimum yearly payments of 1/15th of the initial amount. If you don't make one of these minimum payments, it will be considered income and you will be taxed on it.

Vendor take back; renting with an option to buy; agreement for sale. The next three sections (3, 4 and 5) are complicated and our purpose is only to give you an overview. To explore them in depth you should consult a mortgage expert. Don't let the complications put you off: if schemes like these can get you the property you want, they're certainly worth looking at! (see p. 16). Vendors will consider these three arrangements more often than you might think, especially if the market is dead.

Be sure to have any of these agreements drawn up by a lawyer. The vendor's lawyer usually draws up the documents and it is usually the buyer who pays to have this done. Have all the conditions spelled out clearly in this legal document and have it properly signed and witnessed.

3. VENDOR TAKE BACK.

Situation A: you find a desirable house for $300,000. You have only $60,000 for the down payment and the bank will give you a first mortgage of $160,000 at 9%. You are short $80,000 and the regular financial institutions won't give you a second mortgage.

Solution: the vendor lends you $80,000 (at a mutually agreeable rate) which is secured as a second mortgage on the property. Suppose you agree to have it come due in four years. The title will be transferred to you on the closing date (it will be written right on the title that there is a 'take back' involved).

This is a good deal for you because you get your house. It's a good deal for the vendor because he sells his house and gets a higher rate of interest from you than he would

---

The people often called "lucky" in real estate are usually gutsy, hard-working individuals who have made luck happen.

J. Reinhoffer

---

get from the bank. After four years you will have to either pay off the loan with your own money or renegotiate it.

Situation B: You see a beautiful house, underpriced at $300,000, and you know that you could make money on it. The vendors are anxious to sell and the market is slow. You have only $5,000. The vendors have a first mortgage of $200,000, which is assumable.

The solution: (a) For the down payment the vendors lend you $20,000 at 10% interest. Payments begin immediately and this loan must be repaid within a year. (b) The vendors let you assume the first mortgage because by doing this they avoid the large payout penalty. (c) This leaves $75,000 which the vendors take back as a second mortgage. You've just bought yourself a house! Okay, the monthly payments on two mortgages and a loan might not be easy, but what if the house is a real bargain and you can't help but make money on it when the market turns?

A creative Napa Valley realtor came up with Situation B for a good friend of mine. It's great when you have a realtor who can create such opportunities for you!

4. RENTING WITH AN OPTION TO BUY.

Imagine you see a house you like but can't afford. Offer to rent it for three years at $500 per month above the normal rental price. This might seem like shooting yourself in the foot but it's really an opportunity.

After three years you will have enough equity in the house to equal a down payment:

$500 a month times 3 years (36 months) = $18,000.

It's a longish wait but it's a wise move if it's the only one you can afford. If you rented for these three years in the conventional way, you'd have absolutely nothing to show for your money!

When the lawyer draws up the contract be sure to include the following:

(i) How much of the "inflated" rent will count towards

the purchase. Try to have all of your 'extra' rent money count towards the purchase price, no matter when you end up buying the property.

(ii) What the purchase price will be at the end of the tenancy agreement, i.e. at the end of three years in the example above. Because prices are apt to rise, negotiate a price which is as close as possible to the value of the house as of the beginning of your tenancy. The purchase price must be clearly formulated so that you know how big a mortgage to raise by the end of three years.

(iii) As buyer you must find the mortgage money by the end of the three years. If you can't do this, you forfeit your "extra" rental money and can be evicted without a dime to show for it. On the other hand, as long as you pay the agreed-upon rent, *and providing you have had a proper contract drawn up by a lawyer,* the house cannot be sold from under you.

(iv) The best arrangement from the buyer's point of view is an "option agreement" according to which:

• you can buy the place for $X anytime *before* the three-year period elapses.

• if you can't arrange the financing, (or if you see that house prices are falling . . .) you can walk away without further obligations (or even sell the option agreement to someone else).

Have the lawyer insert a clause stating that if the vendor can't meet his own mortgage payments and/or for whatever reason he's foreclosed on, you'll get all your extra rent money back. Note that a *rent with option to buy* contract is rarely, if ever, registered on the title.

5. AGREEMENT FOR SALE
(wrapping an Agreement for Sale around the existing mortgage).

The vendor already has a mortgage on his place and continues to pay this off. You, the buyer, make a down payment, move in and start making monthly payments (which usually are somewhat more than what the vendor is paying on his mortgage). It is important to arrange for the agreement of sale to come due at the same time that the vendor's mortgage comes up for renewal. On this same date you either assume the mortgage or have your own mortgage in place for the full purchase price.

> *"Money is the most important thing in the world. It represents health, strength, honour, generosity, and beauty as conspicuously as the want of it represents illness, weakness, disgrace, meanness, and ugliness."*
>
> *– George Bernard Shaw*

6. BORROWING ON YOUR EQUITY

This is one of Aqlim's best tips (see pps. 35 and 60) and it is so good that it is worth mentioning again. If you already own property, you have access to instant cash. Many financial institutions will lend you up to 75% of the appraised value of your property less any existing mortgages. This is an excellent way to unlock money which isn't giving you any return and buy that "steal of a deal" which would otherwise slip through your fingers. Putting yourself into debt might seem scary but it is very sensible to go into debt if by doing so you make an excellent investment which also provides a nice little tax write-off.

7. TOTAL CREATIVITY!

This one was suggested to me by Mark Betts, a realtor in White Rock, B.C. I mention it as not only a good plan in itself but as a good example of how creative independent thinking can sometimes provide the answer to your financial problems. It is also an example of the kind of creative resourcefulness you should look for in the realtor whom you choose to work with.

Here's the deal: contact an out-of-town person who owns property in your area and offer to rent the property at about 20% below market value. In exchange for looking after complaints and minor repairs you will have the right to sublet the property. For example, you rent the property for $725 a month, sublet it for $900 and keep the difference of $175. Although this sounds like peanuts, it adds up to $1750 when you're subletting 10 properties. Such cash flow will go a long way to paying off a long-term mortgage on a new property or two which you can now consider buying.

How do you find such properties? It takes time and net-working. Ask realtors for leads (it will be worth a lunch.) Watch for run-down properties, note the addresses and find out the owners' names at the land title office. Watch for ads of houses for rent without a local telephone number. Run your own ad: "Handyman wants to rent house at reduced rent in return for repairs."

8. PARTNERSHIP

a) An investor makes the down payment; you make the mortgage payments. An investor puts up the down payment and the 'buyer' makes the mortgage payments. Both go on title. The investor is bought out at a predetermined date and at a predetermined profit. He is paid either when the house is resold or remortgaged. This works particularly well when one party has ample cash and the other a good income. *(Thanks to Mal Darroch of* Mortgageline *for this idea. Mal tells me that he's seen a number of these arrangements recently. RST)*

b) Protect yourself in a partnership. Go in with a partner or two (see pps. 27, 36) but if you do, be sure to have a *written, witnessed agreement* covering such things as what happens when one person wants to sell and the other doesn't. Writing in the following clause could save you no end of grief (I wish I had known this a few years ago!):

"Any time after a minimum of 18 months from the pur-

"'Knowledge is power.' Nowhere is this truer than in buying real estate."

(Source unknown)

92

chase date either party can demand that the property be professionally evaluated and then demand either (a) that the property be put up for sale and the proceeds split or (b) that the partner who doesn't want to sell, buy the other partner out for half of the appraised value."

OTHER USEFUL TIPS ON MORTGAGES

1. If you own property which you rent out, most financial institutions will let you use half of the rent as part of your qualifying income. When calculating your income it pays to be creative.

2. If one bank won't lend you the money, try another. Then several more. (You might be surprised at the difference between banks.) Try a mortgage broker as well. If even *that* doesn't work, ask a close friend or family member to co-sign for you. Remember Cossman's quote on persistence (p. 33).

Use a mortgage broker. Mortgage brokers are very useful when you're shopping for a mortgage. Many brokers operate as follows: you fill out a mortgage application, the broker feeds this information into his/her computer and faxes it out to many financial institutions. These in turn respond via fax with their best rate. (After all, they are competing for your business.). This saves you a lot of time and haggling. The banks, etc. pay the brokers to provide this service so you pay the broker nothing for this service. Ask your realtor for a good broker or look in the *Yellow Pages* under "Mortgage Brokers."

3. If you want to pay less each month on your mortgage, amortize it over a longer period. The bad news: you will pay much more interest in the long run. The good news: you will have more cash available with which to buy rental properties.

4. On your principal residence, arrange for your mortgage payments to be deducted bi-monthly or even weekly. Mortgage interest on your principal residence is not tax deductible so you should pay the mortgage down as soon as possible.

5. Pre-qualify for a mortgage (see your realtor/ banker/mortgage broker) *before* you make an offer on a house. Pre-qualifying will show the seller that you mean business and don't forget too that from his/her point of view *a bird in the hand is worth two in the bush!* Note that you might pre-qualify and still not get your mortgage because the property must be inspected by the bank and qualify in its own right. Write into your offer that it is subject to an appraisal which satisfies the bank. Give the seller only three business days to complete. If the bank's inspection comes up with a lower figure than the asking price of the house, you have an excellent bargaining chip to obtain a lower price on the house. While you're at it, ask for a package deal on the mortgage, conveyancing, and appraisal fees.

II. INVESTING:

BIG CITIES vs. RURAL COMMUNITIES

BIG CITIES
1. Avoid areas which are overpriced partly because they appeal to the upwardly mobile and/or because buyers seem to be snapping them up no matter what the cost. At the time of this writing (September, 1995) much of Point Grey at the western extremity of Vancouver seems to fall into this category.
2. Areas of a city change, upscaling ("gentrifying") and downscaling. Watch for the signs and try to anticipate these changes. Vancouver's Strathcona area is an interesting case. For years Strathcona was a run-down ghetto. However, this started to change when some adventurous Point Grey residents sold their inflatedly-priced houses and, fortified with large cheques, moved on down to the former ghetto where they started some major overhauling. In the following photo (p. 95) it's not hard to guess which house has had the facelift.

If you drive through Strathcona these days you will see lots of fresh paint, new roofs, vaulted ceilings and skylights. Notice too that the area is conveniently close to the colourful Chinatown market, B.C. and GM Place (the domed stadiums) and the dynamic downtown core of Vancouver (only two kilometers away).

But don't invest in Strathcona on my advice! Check it out yourself first! *Check out anything anyone recommends!* If it's already common knowledge that the demand for houses in a certain area has increased, it's wise to be cautious about buying there. Strathcona is located just south of Hastings and just east of Gore.

RURAL COMMUNITIES
1. Several sensible experts claim there are still underpriced towns outside of Vancouver. Courtenay, Campbell River, Quesnel, Nelson, Cranbrook, Grand Forks, etc. are commonly cited. Advantages: natural beauty, clean air and water, proximity (a few hours' drive) to a major city, lower living expenses (including real estate prices), less crime, friendlier people and a relaxed life style. Be sure to look for a healthy, varied economy so there won't be any shortage of renters.

But where to buy? As usual, it takes research and careful thought: visit rural communities, look at real estate, talk with knowledgeable locals, and read quality publica-

Above: Strathcona, Downtown East Side – spectacular gentrification.

95

tions on real estate. This way you'll pick up gems like the following one by Ozzie Jurock, a Vancouver real estate writer who knows a lot about where to invest. Ozzie says if you're looking for a good town to invest in, you can't go far wrong if you fly on the coat-tails of Walmart, London Drugs, Costco and other big operations. Such companies do their homework and have very good reasons for establishing a new branch in a certain location.

A word of caution. By the time you find out that you should buy in one of these wholesome localities, it may be too late. The hordes might have arrived and pushed the prices out of sight with their demand for property. As we said earlier (page 45), you have to anticipate trends in order to make money.

III. TENANTS AND LANDLORDS
HOT TIPS offers a substantial amount of advice on tenants (pps. 14-15, etc.). Here are some more tips.

CHOOSING TENANTS

1. A telltale sign of a bad news tenant is a messy, dirty vehicle so check out their vehicle before you sign any rental agreement. If their vehicle is a pigsty, why would they treat your suite/house any differently? And, although it may sound old-fashioned, check out their appearance and personal grooming as well. Avoid "shaggy-eared vilains" (Shakespeare).

2. Okay, I'm prejudiced, but I find that certain kinds of 'music' played loudly really jars my nervous apparatus. If you feel the same way, do as I do and set the following

> *"A prospective tenant sometimes looks like Dr. Jekyll at first, but in time begins to take on the appearance of Mr. Hyde."*
>
> *(Source unknown)*

trap. First I ask the prospective tenants how loud they play their music. ('Always soft!' is the inevitable answer!) The naïveté (read: disingenuousness) of this question disarms them and, with some encouragement, they proceed to tell me about the *kind* of music they listen to. If their music falls into a hated category, they don't get in the door because from experience I don't believe that they will play it softly.

3. Screen the prospective tenant carefully. Insist that s/he fill out an application form with references (this includes former landlords and employers). *Definitely check out these references. Immediately.* Proof of employment is crucial. As the old saying goes, "You can't get blood from a stone."

4. It is very wise to fill out a rental agreement (as well as a "Check in, Check out" form: see p. 99). It is possible to buy ready-made rental agreement forms, but the information needed in the agreement is not that complicated so why not save money and draft up your own? Don't forget to make two copies. Cover the following items and you will cover the bases.

RENTAL AGREEMENT FORM
Be sure to include the following:

a. Date and title the document. State that it's an agreement between you and John/Jane Doe. *Phrase it in the following style:*

"This is a rental agreement between John Doe and X ..."

b. What kind of dwelling it is, where it's located. Continue to phrase this as you did in 'a': "The dwelling to be rented is an apartment located at ...")

c. When the tenancy begins, what the rent will be, on what day of the month it is due, and whether you want to charge a late fee (a good idea!).

d. Whether there is a lease. If so, for how long? If not, how much notice do you need? Check on government regulations because they vary. Ditto for the question of raising the rent. Most places have laws dealing with this.

e. The name of someone who is authorized to act for you if you're unavailable.

f. Who is going to rent your place (how many people?) and their names. State clearly if no one other than those listed is to occupy the premises.

g. Who is responsible for paying the utilities.

h. Spell out the exact responsibilities of the landlord, e.g. to keep the appliances in working order, to fix plumbing problems (unless caused by tenant abuse), etc.

i. The exact responsibilities of the tenant(s): for example, not to plug the garburator, or let the lawn go to seed, or flood the bathroom.

j. That the tenant will pay a security deposit and the landlord will hold back only a reasonable amount of this money at the end of the tenancy. The landlord can claim only for damages caused by the tenant and must pay interest on the security deposit.

k. Apart from emergencies, the landlord must get permission in advance in order to enter the rented premises.

l. Iron out the question of subletting: usually permissible subject to the approval of the landlord.

m. Pets. Objectionable pets can also be a problem and maybe it's best not to take them under your roof. It's your choice.* Finding ideal tenants is difficult but it's better to turn away a potential headache than sign one on. You real-

---

A realtor in the West End of Vancouver listed an apartment for sale which neither he nor the owner had seen for 10 months. The realtor phoned the tenant of the apartment to arrange to show the place to a prospective buyer. The tenant seemed polite. A showing time was arranged. The realtor arrived with a prospective buyer. And what did they find? There, in the middle of the living room, on a white carpet, was the biker tenant, rebuilding from scratch, a Harley-Davidson!

---

* We have heard of raccoons, falcons and even alligators kept as pets in the Vancouver area – I do hope the 'gators don't make their way into our lakes because I'm a swimmer . . .

ly don't need the hassle: complaints, damages, pounding noise and bounced cheques.

5. Add a statement that your tenants agree to pay $30 for every bounced cheque and that they will have the carpets professionally steam-cleaned every 12 months. (With this clause they won't be likely to abuse your carpets.) Before they move in, you must receive the final month's rent as a damage deposit.

6. If you want to add to this rental agreement, check out some that are on the market. If you cover the above points, you will have a viable document. Again, check out those references and have the signing witnessed.

The CHECK IN, CHECK OUT form. Inspect the premises with the tenant and make a list of all damages (include carpet stains and dents in the walls). Both parties sign this form when it's completed. Have it witnessed. These steps are very important. Use this same form when the tenant vacates.

7. Save money on any repairs by asking carpet cleaners, tilers, carpenters, cabinetmakers, mirror salespeople, miniblind sellers, plumbers, etc. for a "professional's discount." Squeaky wheel gets the grease!

8. Lease or rental agreement? A lease is a two-edged sword: it nails down the tenants but also makes it hard to get rid of them. What if you hear of a bargain house? On the other hand, a rental agreement is absolutely necessary because it spells out what each of you is agreeing to.

IV. OVERALL STRATEGY – WHEN TO BUY

1. The Golden Rule: Sell when things are booming and lots of people are buying. This takes guts to do because prices are rising! Turn a blind eye! Buy in a slump when few people are buying. Also hard to do because prices are falling and you think they might keep falling . . . Many people make sheep-like bleats and follow the herd like well-trained sheep: do not listen to them! Ditto for the media: if you hear it in the media you're probably too late! Read and listen to quality information (See pages 110 - 112.)

2. Use the "listing to sold ratio." Apply the following formula to the area you're interested in, and you will get a pretty accurate indication of whether real estate prices are going to increase or decrease. Here's how it works: *Divide the number of houses listed at the beginning of the current month* (consult the MLS "Listings" book) *by the number of houses which sold in the same area last month* (consult the MLS "Sales" book for last month). This gives you the number of months' supply of houses.

Here's what these books look like:

MLS Listings book   MLS Sales book

To continue with our example, here are the current (September 25, 1995) figures for North Vancouver:

402 houses for sale in North Van. (on Sept. 1/95) ÷ 132 houses sold in North Van. (in August, 1995)

Divide 132 into 402 and you get 3.05, which is the number of months' supply of houses in North Vancouver.

When the supply goes under 4.0 prices tend to rise. When the supply goes over 4.0 prices tend to fall. When the supply goes under three months, buy. When the supply goes over six months, sell. Classic supply and demand stuff. Very useful to know!

LEVERAGE

1. The more units you own, the more leverage (money-making potential) you have. If you buy one apartment for $100,000, your equity will (sooner or later) increase by X. If you buy four units, putting $25,000 down on each, your equity will increase by 4X. Make sure your rents are covering expenses and sell off any unit which is becoming bothersome, e.g. hard to rent out or causing a large monthly shortfall.

> *"Give me a lever big enough and I will move the earth itself."*
>
> *– Archimedes, 220 B.C.*

2. Within reason, make your down payments as small as possible. Amortize over the longest possible period (the maximum in Canada is 30 years). This will keep your monthly mortgage payments low. Try to have some money on hand for emergency repairs and for that "steal of a deal" which might come up.

IN GENERAL

1. This is a repeat but it can hardly be said often enough: Do your research and *know* when you're looking at a good deal! Then make low offers.

2. Keep informed. Be aware of interest rates and whether housing prices are stable, rising or falling. Think of selling a place or two when prices seem to be rising.

3. Houses (and duplexes) usually cost more than apartments but they'll make you more money.

V. ON BUYING THAT SPECIAL HOUSE:

Preview of Godwin Books' next release,

"HOT TIPS FOR THE HOME BUYER."

GODWIN BOOKS will be publishing (probably in late 1995) a detailed book on how to buy a house *systematically.*

About 60 pages. Illustrated. To give you a preview, here are a few (simplified) extracts on:
(a) fine-tuning your offer (a short-cut); and
(b) how to choose the right realtor (from the *buyer's* point of view).

(a) A shortcut for fine-tuning your offer:

i. Find out the assessed value of the house then calculate 95% of this figure. Find out the *lowest recent sale* of a comparable house in the neighborhood where the house you're bidding on is located. Your realtor should be able to get this information.

ii. The average of these two figures should represent a shrewd opening offer. Naturally you'll allow for significant differences between the house you're bidding on and the house you're using as a comparable.

iii. Find out how much the vendor paid for the house, when s/he bought it and why s/he is selling it. Weigh this information in the light of a historical graph of median house prices in the area. Think about the vendor's situation and motives.

iv. Fine-tune this figure with your own intuitive sense of local property values (and you will have seen so many comparables by this point that there won't be much guesswork to this operation!) and, daring to err on the low side, choose your price for a starting offer. The importance of making low offers cannot be overestimated. Psych yourself up to do it!

In the future, all MLS listings will probably be accessible via home computer. For the moment, only NRS Block Bros. offers this service. You can pick up a floppy disk from any Block Bros. office, take it home, and check out their listings. Ask for their "HOUSE BY MOUSE." Keep informed: things change constantly.

(b)   Choosing a realtor (from the *buyer's* perspective).
Besides other qualities, a good realtor really knows property values, is among the first to discover good listings (often via his/her own personal computer), and is genuinely interested in finding the best possible deal for his/her client. Such a realtor is a valuable ally and an invaluable source of money-making information and is worth every cent of the commission.

When you choose a realtor, choose someone who:

• is genuine, sincere, truthful, hard-working and intelligent.

• listens well, especially as you attempt to clarify the kind of house you are looking for. This can take time.

• keeps you informed swiftly (preferably by fax) about promising listings. Contacts you *regularly.*

• gives you what you need to survive in the MARKET JUNGLE. For example, my realtor lets me consult his MLS "Sales" book. This is a great way to get an overview of the market and an idea of the reality of prices. It is also a good tool for setting your own price parameters.

• is creative and knowledgeable about financing and even has a network of useful people in this field.

To pull your weight in working with such a realtor, as the buyer you should:

• be genuine, sincere, truthful, etc.

• be *loyal* and make it clear to other realtors that you already have a commitment. *Remember this at the open houses you might attend on your own.*

• keep in touch. Keep your realtor informed about what you've discovered in *your* search, whether your ideas on what you're looking for have evolved, (and if so, in what way), whether you've decided you're no longer really serious about a house. In short, *communicate.*

• collaborate in the search: listen well and read the information your realtor gives you. Try to understand the market from his/her perspective.

Below you will find a long and a short checklist for keeping track of those houses you look at. Tailor each list to suit your own needs (delete, change, or add). Then photocopy a bunch and put them on a clipboard.

These lists are very useful. They will help you to focus, to get the right information, to remember what you've seen, to compare and discuss the houses you've seen. They are an important part of becoming an expert on house prices.

Good luck in your hunting! Here's the short form:

SHORT FORM CHECKLIST

1. ADDRESS: _____
    _____

2. TYPE OF HOUSE _____
    (HERITAGE, NEW ENGLAND, RANCHER, ETC.

3. WHEN BUILT (YEAR): _____

4. TYPE OF NEIGHBORHOOD: _____
    (CROWDED, 'CLASSY,' TREED, BARREN, ETC.)

5. VIEW OR NOT? VIEW OF WHAT?_____

6. ASKING PRICE: $ _____

7. IMPRESSION AS TO ITS TRUE WORTH: $_____

8. HOW LONG HAS IT BEEN ON THE MARKET? _____

9. WHY IS IT BEING SOLD?_____
    _____

10. SQUARE FOOTAGE OF HOUSE (UP AND DOWN): _____

11. BEDROOMS (HOW MANY?) _____

12. LIVING ROOM (BIG ENOUGH? VAULTED? ETC.)_____

13. KITCHEN (BIG ENOUGH? MODERN ENOUGH? ETC.) _____
    _____

14. BATHROOMS (HOW MANY): _____

15. FIREPLACES?_____

16. HOW DO YOU RATE THE HOUSE ON A SCALE OF 1-10?_____

17. NAME OF REAL ESTATE CONTACT PERSON: _____
    _____

RATING OUT OF 10:__
HOUSE PROFILE CHECKLIST

1. ADDRESS: _____

2. KIND OF HOUSE _____
   (HERITAGE, NEW ENGLAND, RANCHER, ETC.)

3. WHEN BUILT (YEAR) _____

4. TYPE OF NEIGHBORHOOD: _____
   (SPACIOUS/CROWDED, 'CLASSY'/RUN-DOWN, TREED/BARREN,
   MANICURED/GONE TO SEED, ETC.)

5. LOCATION (NEAR AMENITIES? _____
   TOO ISOLATED? NOISY STREET OR PLAYGROUND? _____

6. VIEW OR NOT? VIEW OF WHAT? _____

7. OVERALL ATTRACTIVENESS OF THE HOUSE: _____

8. ASKING PRICE: _____

9. IMPRESSION AS TO ITS TRUE WORTH: _____

10. HOW LONG HAS IT BEEN ON THE MARKET? _____

11. WHY IS IT BEING SOLD? _____

12. LAST SOLD FOR: _____

13. DATE IT LAST SOLD: _____
    WHAT WAS MARKET LIKE THEN? _____

14. SALES OF RECENT COMPARABLE PROPERTY IN THE
    NEIGHBORHOOD? _____

15. ANY ASSUMABLE MORTGAGES? DETAILS: _____
    _____

16. TAXES: $ _____

17. SQUARE FOOTAGE OF HOUSE (UP AND DOWN): _____

18. SIZE OF LOT: _____

19. BEDROOMS (HOW MANY?) _____

20. LIVING ROOM (BIG ENOUGH? VAULTED? ETC.) _____

21. DINING ROOM? _____

22. KITCHEN (BIG ENOUGH? MODERN ENOUGH? ETC.) _____
    _____

23. BATHROOMS (HOW MANY?) _____
    OFF MASTER BEDROOM? _____

24. FIREPLACES? _____

25. STORAGE SPACE? _____

26. GARAGE? (COVERED? CARPORT? ETC. _____

27. GENERAL CONDITION (ROOF, PLUMBING, CONDITION OF CARPETS, FURNACE, ETC.) _____

    WHEN LAST SERVICED?_____

28. DOES THE HOUSE CONTAIN A RENTABLE SUITE (OR DOES IT HAVE THE POTENTIAL FOR DEVELOPING A SUITE?) _____

29. IF IT ALREADY CONTAINS A SUITE, HOW MUCH REVENUE DOES IT BRING IN? $ _____

30. ANY SIGN OF THE TENANTS, WHETHER THEY'D BE GOOD OR BAD, WHETHER THEY'D WANT TO STAY ON?_____

31. HOW MANY OF YOUR MAIN CRITERIA DOES THE HOUSE SATISFY? _____

32. IS THE HOUSE DEFICIENT IN ANY MAJOR CRITERIA? OVERALL 'FEEL' OF THE HOUSE (PEACEFUL/ CLUTTERED/ EXPOSED ETC.) _____

    NOTES _____

    _____
    _____
    _____
    _____
    _____

MAKE A GAME OF IT! If you are looking for houses with a partner, it's more fun if you share the tasks: one person reads some ads to the other, then you switch; when you've mapped out your house-hunting expedition, one person drives, the other acts as navigator.

HOW TO FOCUS
MY PERSONAL REAL ESTATE
INVESTMENT PLAN

A. MY PERSONAL GOAL IS TO MAKE $_____
   BY INVESTING IN REAL ESTATE.

B. I PLAN TO ACHIEVE THIS GOAL BY THE FOLLOWING DATE:

_____

C. I AM INTERESTED IN THOROUGHLY RESEARCHING THE
   FOLLOWING GEOGRAPHICAL AREAS:

D. THE TYPE OF HOUSING WHICH INTERESTS ME THE MOST IS
   (CHECK FROM THE FOLLOWING: ____ HOUSES, ____ DUPLEXES,
   ____ TRIPLEXES, ____ TOWNHOUSES, ____ APARTMENTS,
   ____ LAND, ____ RESIDENTIAL, ____ RECREATIONAL, ETC.)

E. THE PRICE PARAMETERS WHICH I WANT TO SET ARE UNDER
   (FILL IN YOUR OWN: $350,000 OR WHATEVER) $ _____

F. IN ORDER TO BECOME AN EXPERT IN THIS NICHE OF THE
   MARKET I AM GOING TO DO THE FOLLOWING:

FIND A GOOD REALTOR

1. FIND A REALTOR WHO:

- IS INTELLIGENT AND HARD-WORKING (HIS/HER SALES
  RECORD WILL BE A TIP-OFF).
- IS COMPUTER-LITERATE. YOU NEED TO BE INFORMED AS SOON
  AS A HOT DEAL POPS UP ON THE REALTOR'S RESIDENTIAL
  COMPUTER SCREEN (AND THAT'S WHERE THEY FIRST APPEAR).
- SOMEONE I FEEL I CAN TRUST.
- REREAD PPS. 35, 103 OF "HOT TIPS (REVISED)" FOR MORE
  CRITERIA.
- INTERVIEW AT LEAST TWO REALTORS.
- ASK FOR WRITTEN TESTIMONIALS, EVEN PHONE NUMBERS,
  OF SATISFIED CLIENTS FOR WHOM THEY *FOUND* (NOT SOLD)
  A HOUSE.

- MAYBE SHARE YOUR GOALS WITH THESE APPLICANTS.
- MY REALTOR OF CHOICE IS:

_____

THE SEARCH

2. START DRIVING AROUND YOUR GEOGRAPHI-CAL AREA, NOTING PROMISING HOUSES
(WITH LISTING REALTOR'S NAME AND TELEPHONE NUMBER).

- PHONE THESE REALTORS. GET MORE INFORMATION (PREFERABLY BY FAX IF YOU NEED INTERIOR PHOTOS AND/OR COMPARABLES, ETC.). EITHER TOSS OUT OR VIEW.
- FILL OUT A CHECKLIST FOR EACH HOUSE VIEWED. (THIS IS A VITAL STEP IN BECOMING PROFICIENT IN PRICING).
- KEEP THESE CHECKLISTS IN A LOGBOOK (3-HOLE PUNCHED). USE EITHER THE SHORT OR LONG FORM, MAYBE BOTH, DEPENDING ON YOUR LEVEL OF INTEREST IN THE HOUSE.

I/WE VIEWED FROM THIS SOURCE_____HOUSES IN THE FIRST MONTH.

3. LOOK IN THE WANT ADS AND REAL ESTATE WEEKLIES FOR PROMISING HOUSES.

- PHONE LISTING REALTORS FOR MORE INFORMATION. IF NEED BE, HAVE THEM FAX YOU MORE INFORMATION.
- ARRANGE TO VIEW AT LEAST FOUR PER WEEK.
- MAKE CLEAR TO LISTING REALTORS THE NAME OF THE REALTOR THAT YOU ARE WORKING WITH. THIS IS VITAL BECAUSE YOU DON'T WANT YOUR REALTOR TO LOSE HIS/HER COMMISSION. THEY ARE PART OF YOUR TEAM.
- FILL OUT A CHECKLIST FOR EACH HOUSE VIEWED.

I/WE VIEWED FROM THIS SOURCE_____HOUSES IN THE FIRST MONTH.

4. ATTEND A MINIMUM OF____ OPEN HOUSES PER WEEK AND KEEP A RECORD OF WHAT YOU SEE AT THESE OPENS IN YOUR LOG BOOK.

I/WE VIEWED FROM THIS SOURCE_____HOUSES IN THE FIRST MONTH.

TOTAL NUMBER OF HOUSES VIEWED IN FIRST MONTH: _____

· AS MENTIONED EARLIER (P. 104) THE CHECKLIST WILL HELP YOU TO ASK THE RIGHT QUESTIONS, SYSTEMATICALLY. WITHIN A MONTH OR SO YOU SHOULD BE PRETTY COMPETENT IN HOUSE PRICES FOR YOUR AREA, TYPE OF HOUSING AND PRICE PARAMETERS. YOUR REALTOR SHOULD BE A GOOD GUIDE BUT I RECOMMEND THAT YOU TOO BECOME A BIT OF A PRICE EXPERT. IF YOU DO, IF YOU KNOW WITHIN ABOUT 5% WHAT A GIVEN HOUSE IS REALLY WORTH, YOU WILL BE IN A POSITION TO MAKE A VERY ASTUTE LOW OFFER ON A HOUSE.
- SEE PAGE 102 FOR THE KEY POINTS ON HOW TO PITCH THAT ALL-IMPORTANT OPENING OFFER.

G. IN ORDER TO RAISE MONEY FOR MY FIRST (OR NEXT) HOUSE PURCHASE, I HAVE THE FOLLOWING PLAN.

1. GET MY DOWN PAYMENT READY. REVIEW PAGES 86-92 OF "HOT TIPS REVISED" FOR CREATIVE IDEAS, E.G. CMHC'S 5% PLAN (PAGE 87).
- ESTIMATE OF AMOUNT NEEDED: $ _____

- WHICH BANKING INSTITUTIONS TO APPROACH FOR THE MONEY (AND DON'T FORGET TO BARGAIN . . .)

_____

_____

2. IF I DECIDE TO SHARE THE COST OF BUYING A HOUSE, _____ APPROACH THE FOLLOWING PEOPLE ABOUT A PARTNERSHIP (SEE P. 92 AND "PARTNERSHIP" IN INDEX OF THIS BOOK):

_____

_____

3. GET MY MORTGAGE IN PLACE. SEE THE FOLLOWING BROKERS (DON'T FORGET TO GET THE MORTGAGE PREAPPROVED AND DON'T FORGET TO BARGAIN)

_____

_____

H. MAKE THE INITIAL BID ON THAT HOUSE. REREAD PAGE 102. DON'T FORGET TO MAKE THE OFFER TO BUY SUBJECT TO A HOUSE INSPECTION.

GOOD HUNTING!

Good publications to read in order to understand what's happening in the world of real estate.

There is so much printed about real estate every day that it is tempting to ignore it all and read nothing. However, if you're going to invest, it would be very unwise to imitate the ostrich. A wiser course is to limit yourself to a few *quality* publications. I highly recommend Ozzie Jurock and David Ingram. Both writers are well-informed, have lots of experience and a knack for seeing through the clutter and *conventional wisdom* to the essence of the matter. Both seem to be pretty independent, i.e. non-affiliated and objective. Apart from the knowledge that you gain from writers like these, there is an intangible bonus to reading them: you learn to think and analyze in much the same way that they do.

Jurock's newsletter is a distillation of many good sources – national and international – and from it you learn a great deal about both arenas. Here are two passages to illustrate. Notice that in (a) Jurock deals with the international scene (and its impact locally) while in (b) he analyzes the local (Vancouver) real estate market. This is valuable information.

(a) "Why would the dollar fall to 60 cents? It is simple. If Quebec leaves Canada, the risk increases substantially that Canadians and Quebeckers alike might default on their internationally-held public debt." (p. 16) or this: (b) "In Vancouver the developers' pain (overbuilding of condos) has resulted in some very nice condo deals out there for owner/occupiers. (As an investor, be extremely picky and buy only with the resale buyer in mind. There's a lot of stuff out there, which means slower if any appreciation and lots of desperate competition when it comes to that resale.)" (p. 6, Sept./Oct. 1995.)

Ingram is also useful. The following is typical of his writing:

(1) "There are two main reasons to buy RRSP's: to save taxes now and to provide for the future. What many peo-

ple don't realize is that they may actually be increasing their total taxes and will have less in the future than with other investments. (. . .) When you withdraw your money it will be taxed at the prevailing rates." *Investment Guide,* p. 130.

(2) "While it is true that real estate keeps pace with inflation, it does not necessarily keep in sync with inflation. The price of a standard two storey house in North Toronto jumped by almost 36% in 1988 compared to the CPI (Consumer Price Index) of around 4.5% for Canada. In Winnipeg, the sale price of the same house dropped by about 2.5%." *Investment Guide,* p. 134.

Although HOT TIPS deals with Greater Vancouver and although both Jurock and Ingram both live here, their publications will be useful to you no matter where you live. Having said that, *if you don't live in B.C. I recommend that you check out your local scene for writers of similar quality.* Some of the best (i.e. most original, most uninhibited

Jurock's Newsletter

Ingram's book

by editorial policy) writers in Canada and the U.S.A. work for small, local, independent publications.

For information about Jurock's monthly *Newsletter,* phone 604-683-1111 or fax 683-1707. Ask for a free sample. A year's subscription costs $295. To contact David Ingram, phone 604-980-0321 or fax 649-4759. Ingram's book *Investment Guide* costs $14.95. His *CEN-TA-PEDE NEWSLET-*

TER costs $125 a year. Free samples available.

Business In Vancouver is also useful. This Vancouver-based weekly contains excellent articles on many aspects of business, including real estate, and if real estate's your thing you're more likely to do well if you have knowledge of the total business environment. The following extracts will show you what I mean.

(1) "Elaine Cheung, president of Asia West Properties (. . .) clinched the deal last week for The Nelson Towers, at an estimated $15 million. The new owners chose this building over several buildings in Kitsilano and the West End because in Metrotown (Burnaby) a significant amount of new commercial development and condo construction is expected to lead to future rent increases and capital appreciation of properties."

Or this: (2) "To sell effectively to Asians, observe and respect Asian cultures. In Chinese culture, physical contact such as a firm handshake and a slap to the shoulder may be considered insulting."

Phone 604-688-2398 or fax 688-1963 and you will receive a free copy of *Business In Vancouver*. A year's subscription costs $64.

Business in Vancouver

> *There were over 1,000 foreclosures listed in the Vancouver Court Registry last year (1995).*

I wasn't going to include foreclosures in this edition of *Hot Tips* but you hear so much about them in the media that I changed my mind. I'm not convinced foreclosures are an easy way to make big bucks in real estate. True, you can get lucky and just happen to hear of a great deal (especially if you get your network working with you) but this is unlikely. To make money buying a foreclosure you probably will have to do careful research, just as you would in buying a house on the real estate market.

To try your hand at foreclosures, here's the scoop. Check out the newspaper (the "real estate" section of the classifieds) or ask a few realtors. If you do hear of a promising deal, go to the local courthouse ("registry" section) in order to get the information you need. You have to know the reference number (e.g. H950270). You'll pay a $4.00 fee for the right to peruse this file on the courthouse premises.

Note the name and address of the owners (there will be no telephone number – it's against the law to list one) and send them a letter of enquiry. Would they be interested in selling? Could you have a closer look at the house? If you don't hear from the owners soon, send a follow-up letter a few weeks later.

If you want to look into foreclosures more systematically, find out if anyone where you live is marketing this information. In Vancouver (and B.C.) try *Ideal Source Publishing.* They sell lists of foreclosures complete with the assessed value of the house and will send you free of charge a sample weekly list. Tel. 604-327-7595; fax 327-7517. They will keep you supplied for a year for $475 (mail) or $425 (fax). For Calif. foreclosures tel. 1-800-310-7730.

If you work from this kind of list, look for the following:

1. Signs of a marital break-up (watch for separate addresses).

2. Second and third mortgages (these will be listed under "Additional respondents").

3. The number of days until the owner actually will lose possession.

Foreclosures are a sad business but look at it this way: if you cut a deal with the owner, you'll be doing him/ her a favor because from his/her point of view the ultimate nightmare is to see that house seized by the bank!

No doubt it takes considerable practice to recognize which properties on the list are worth investigating. In general, it is probably best to stick with properties close to home. And, as usual, before you decide you're interested in a given house, *do your research.* How much did the owner buy it for? What has comparable property sold for recently, i.e. what is the house really worth on the current market? Then make your offer, possibly at 20% below the market value (see page 102).

"Economics used to be called 'the dismal science.' It may be dismal but there is something even more dismal and that is to remain ignorant of how profitable real estate can be and to spend the rest of your life paying rent to someone."

(Robert Courtenay Hoare)

INDEX

We wish to thank the following for their time and valuable information:

For all-round assistance:

DR. GLORIA BURIMA,
North Vancouver

MR. RICK ANDERSON
Real Estate Editor, *North Shore News*

MS. KAY FOERSTER
Kai-more Administration Services
Tel. 986-7555

For help with the section on mortgages and how to raise money for real estate investment:

MR. JOHN SCOTT
Canada Trust
Tel. 220-5501

MR. MAL DARROCH
MortgageLine,
Tel. 662-7007

MR. MICHAEL FREIMARK
The Mortgage Source
Tel. 582-7121

MR. BYARD WOOD
Canadian Home Income Plan
Tel. 1-800-563-2447

MR. RICK POTTIN
Vanquest Real Estate Corp.
Tel. 669-9839

MS. NADINE STAUNTON
Canada Trust, Surrey
Tel. 581-1919

Also thanks for creative ideas to:

MR. MARK BETTS
Realtor, Hugh and McKinnon,
Tel. 604-531-1909

MR. CAM FOSTER
Realty World in Town,
West end of Vancouver.

MR. TED STAUNTON
Sherwood Graphics (text formatting)
Tel. 582-6729

A fine gift for those who appreciate
B.C.'s heritage

"THE ETERNAL FOREST"

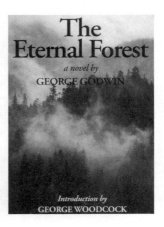

by George Godwin (1889-1974)

Preface by George Woodcock

Vancouver real estate took a beating in 1981. George Godwin would not have been surprised at this because he had already analyzed first-hand the big boom-bust of 1912-13. Here's his description of Vancouver in 1912:

"The mad boom was without economic justification; there was no big business to back it. Grandview came on the market during this boom time and so did many other undeveloped suburbs. Lots changed hands four, five and six times a day. Men dealt in them as men deal in groceries. It was the only business being done in the city." (p. 139.)

Or how's this for a description of a Douglas fir . . .

The alders were felled easily but the giant Douglas firs were no such easy game. Their corrugated trunks, fluted from base to summit, symmetrical as Corinthian columns, soared up into the sky and spread branches like dark and velvety fans against the leaden sky. Against these the axe became a pigmy tool wielded by a pigmy hewer. (p. 34.)

This book is a mystery. It is also a major discovery for Canadian literature. Godwin wrote about the Vancouver of 1912-16 but much of what he says sounds eerily like the present. He's our answer to Alexis de Toqueville.

What the critics have said:

"What a surprise this novel is! It is written with white-hot outrage at hypocrisy and double-dealing" – *B.C. Bookworld, summer 1995.*

"Every page is a sculpted masterpiece . . . reminiscent of Ford Maddox Ford" – *Victoria Times-Colonist.*

"Godwin writes with . . . an appreciation of the enduring spiritual value of woods and wilderness. (. . .) He has a very good sociological understanding of early B.C." – *B.C. Studies.*

Enclose $17.95 softcover, $29.95 hardcover if in Canada. We pay the postage and GST. U.S. prices are $14.95 (soft), $23.95 (hard). See the ad on *Italian for the Opera* (next page) on how to order.

How to order "Hot Tips For Real Estate Investors" through the mail

1. Make out a cheque to 'Godwin Books' for $10.95. Only $10.95. Do not add anything for GST or postage. We will take care of these.
2. Send the cheque to P.O. Box 4781, Vancouver, B.C. V6B 4A4, Canada.
3. Within one day we will take action and will send you a copy of "Hot Tips," by first class postage and securely packaged.
4. Please state if you would like the author to sign your copy.
5. A discount of 10% is available for 2-5 orders. (If you want 5 copies enclose 5 x $10.95 – 10% = $49.00.) A discount of 20% is available for 6 copies or more. (If you want 10 copies, enclose 10 x $10.95 – 20% = $87.60.)
6. To U.S. customers: deduct 10% from Canadian amounts. *Our tel. no. is 604 988 2407*

Robert S. Thomson, Ph.D., Editor, Godwin Books

SHORT FORM CHECKLIST

1. ADDRESS:_____
   _____

2. TYPE OF HOUSE _____
   (HERITAGE, NEW ENGLAND, RANCHER, ETC.

3. WHEN BUILT (YEAR): _____

4. TYPE OF NEIGHBORHOOD: _____
   (CROWDED, 'CLASSY,' TREED, BARREN, ETC.)

5. VIEW OR NOT? VIEW OF WHAT?_____

6. ASKING PRICE: $ _____

7. IMPRESSION AS TO ITS TRUE WORTH: $_____

8. HOW LONG HAS IT BEEN ON THE MARKET? _____

9. WHY IS IT BEING SOLD?_____
   _____

10. SQUARE FOOTAGE OF HOUSE (UP AND DOWN): _____

11. BEDROOMS (HOW MANY?) _____

12. LIVING ROOM (BIG ENOUGH? VAULTED? ETC.)_____

13. KITCHEN (BIG ENOUGH? MODERN ENOUGH? ETC.) _____
    _____

14. BATHROOMS (HOW MANY): _____

15. FIREPLACES?_____

16. HOW DO YOU RATE THE HOUSE ON A SCALE OF 1-10?_____

17. NAME OF REAL ESTATE CONTACT PERSON: _____
    _____

RATING OUT OF 10:___
HOUSE PROFILE CHECKLIST

1. ADDRESS: _____

2. KIND OF HOUSE _____
   (HERITAGE, NEW ENGLAND, RANCHER, ETC.)

3. WHEN BUILT (YEAR) _____

4. TYPE OF NEIGHBORHOOD: _____
   (SPACIOUS/CROWDED, 'CLASSY'/RUN-DOWN, TREED/BARREN,
   MANICURED/GONE TO SEED, ETC.)

5. LOCATION (NEAR AMENITIES?_____
   TOO ISOLATED? NOISY STREET OR PLAYGROUND?_____

6. VIEW OR NOT? VIEW OF WHAT? _____

7. OVERALL ATTRACTIVENESS OF THE HOUSE: _____

8. ASKING PRICE: _____

9. IMPRESSION AS TO ITS TRUE WORTH: _____

10. HOW LONG HAS IT BEEN ON THE MARKET? _____

11. WHY IS IT BEING SOLD? _____

12. LAST SOLD FOR: _____

13. DATE IT LAST SOLD: _____
    WHAT WAS MARKET LIKE THEN? _____

14. SALES OF RECENT COMPARABLE PROPERTY IN THE
    NEIGHBORHOOD?_____

15. ANY ASSUMABLE MORTGAGES? DETAILS: _____
    _____

16. TAXES: $_____

17. SQUARE FOOTAGE OF HOUSE (UP AND DOWN): _____

18. SIZE OF LOT:_____

19. BEDROOMS (HOW MANY?)_____

20. LIVING ROOM (BIG ENOUGH? VAULTED? ETC.) _____

21. DINING ROOM? _____

22. KITCHEN (BIG ENOUGH? MODERN ENOUGH? ETC.)_____
    _____

23. BATHROOMS (HOW MANY?) _____
    OFF MASTER BEDROOM?_____

24. FIREPLACES? _____

25. STORAGE SPACE? _____

26. GARAGE? (COVERED? CARPORT? ETC. _____

27. GENERAL CONDITION (ROOF, PLUMBING, CONDITION OF CARPETS, FURNACE, ETC.) _____

    WHEN LAST SERVICED? _____

28. DOES THE HOUSE CONTAIN A RENTABLE SUITE (OR DOES IT HAVE THE POTENTIAL FOR DEVELOPING A SUITE?) _____

29. IF IT ALREADY CONTAINS A SUITE, HOW MUCH REVENUE DOES IT BRING IN? $ _____

30. ANY SIGN OF THE TENANTS, WHETHER THEY'D BE GOOD OR BAD, WHETHER THEY'D WANT TO STAY ON? _____

31. HOW MANY OF YOUR MAIN CRITERIA DOES THE HOUSE SATISFY? _____

32. IS THE HOUSE DEFICIENT IN ANY MAJOR CRITERIA? OVERALL 'FEEL' OF THE HOUSE (PEACEFUL/ CLUTTERED/ EXPOSED ETC.) _____

    NOTES _____

    _____

    _____

    _____

    _____

    _____

NOTES

NOTES